BAKING BREAD AT HOME

Traditional Recipes from Around the World

BAKING BREAD AT HOME

Traditional Recipes from Around the World

TOM JAINE

PHOTOGRAPHS BY
JACQUI HURST

CASSELLPAPERBACKS

First published in 1995 by George Weidenfeld & Nicolson Ltd

First published in paperback in 1997 by Phoenix Illustrated

This paperback edition first published in 2001 by
Cassell Paperbacks, Cassell & Co
Wellington House, 125 Strand
London, WC2R 0BB

Distributed in the United States of America by
Sterling Publishing Co., Inc.
387 Park Avenue South,
New York, NY 10016-8810

British Library Cataloguing-in-Publication Data
A catalogue record for this book is available from
the British Library

ISBN 184188166X

Edited by Felicity Jackson
Designed by Thumb Design
Printed and bound in Italy

CONTENTS

BREAD PAST AND PRESENT

Bread is a staple food, and has been ever since the time when man ceased hunting game and gathering wild plants and took instead to sowing crops and harvesting them. Not every society in the world grew wheat and its relatives, the essential ingredient for bread: more people depend on rice, for example, than on wheat; and the whole of North and Central America, before European discovery, grew corn.

However, for those who lived in the Middle East, north Asia, and Europe, bread was essential. As history has turned out, it is from these regions that some of the great modern migrations—of peoples, political power, and economic influence—have originated.

Throughout all of these great historical changes, bread has traveled in the saddlepack, so that it, too, has colonized great tracts of the Americas, Africa, Australia, and south Asia.

Watching the making of a simple chapati, or the mass production of a loaf of white bread, we take for granted some tremendous leaps of human invention and discovery, each in their way as momentous as the capturing of fire and heat, and as lost in the mists of time.

Breadmaking requires flour; to get flour one needs a mill and a field full of grain, which calls for agriculture and sophisticated grinding technology. Risen bread requires yeasts, which must have taken centuries of haphazard trial and error to tame and make reliable. And, finally, baking requires ovens, no small detail.

Without each of these steps, any one of which speaks of generations of development, we are left with simple porridges and gruels—grains mixed with water and boiled.

Even a Mexican tortilla, the griddle bread made from cornmeal by the Aztecs and the Maya, now spread through fast-food outlets in the USA and in Europe, conceals infinite pains. It seems easy to make a flat disk of cornmeal and cook it quickly on a hotplate. Yet to achieve this, the ancient Mexican peoples had to devise a way to treat kernels of corn with limewater to soften the husks, and boil the starch to make a fresh paste that could be converted into paper-thin tortillas. They also discovered that if they dried this paste, they could regrind it into a flour that would keep all winter long—and that, too, would make tortillas. Bread is not as simple as it seems.

16th-century French woodcut showing a baker with his ovens. In the background, on the left, an apprentice is loading an oven with raised pies; the baker himself is using his peel to load small rolls, perhaps manchets, while larger round loaves are rising in the warmth of the oven on the right. His immediate helper can be seen weighing pieces of dough for the rolls and molding them into balls two-handed—just as molding is done today.

GRAINS

Bread cannot be made without some flour: wheat, rye, barley, or oats, the four essentials that have been grown in Europe and Asia for this purpose—with wheat the king—though pea and bean flour, chestnut, rice, and potato have also been used to expand options in times of famine, not to mention breads made with tree bark or acorns.

The grains that are harvested today are the result of much care. Ancient farmers were not so lucky, making do with primitive forms—single-row barley, emmer, einkorn, and spelt, the latter still grown in marginal climates—from which we have selected and refined certain characteristics.

WHEAT

The most effective grain for breadmaking is wheat, not only because it tastes good—with a certain nuttiness, no bitterness, and a round, sometimes rich flavor—but because it performs well. An ear of wheat has all the ingredients for a good loaf: starch to give bulk, feed the yeasts, and turn a lovely golden brown in the oven; germ to lend essential fats and oils, and improve bread's nutritional value; bran to lend weight and help our digestion; and gluten, that magic component possessed by wheat more than any other grain, which lets the loaf stretch and rise to perfection.

Wheats vary from one breed, one harvest, and one location to another. Gluten, which is a protein, is one of the essential variants. Wheats grown in hot, dry summers over a short season, i.e. sown in the spring and harvested three or four months later, contain more protein than those from cooler places, where crops may be sown in the winter to give a better chance of ripening. Hence wheat from the prairies of North America, the plains of Hungary in Central Europe, the northern provinces of India, or Australia is particularly blessed with protein. This is called hard wheat, and it makes a strong flour. The gluten content is high, and loaves rise better and are lighter.

European wheats, with the exception of the durum wheats in Italy used for pastamaking, are mainly softer, producing weaker flour. A soft flour is ideal for making pastry and cakes, in which a chewy texture is undesirable. When bread is made with soft wheat, it will tend to be denser and less refined. The big advantage of soft wheat, however, is its flavor. It simply has more. The hearty country loaves of France illustrate these

points perfectly. But when a French baker wanted something more dainty, he would often use imported flour.

The position today has been changed by chemists and agricultural science. European wheats, through careful breeding, are no longer as soft as they were; and bakers and millers can alter their performance by adding pure gluten and other improvers. When you use a bag of 100% American strong flour, you can see the remarkable properties of spring wheat from the prairies.

A selection of the flours available for making bread. Top row, left to right: 85% wheatmeal, 100% organic wholewheat, unbleached all-purpose, white bread flour. Bottom row left to right: commeal or polenta, barley flour, organic rye, chapati flour.

OTHER GRAINS

Rye is an excellent bread flour. It has a fine flavor, and sufficient gluten (although not very much) to rise in the making. Rye loaves will always be denser than wheaten, and nowadays almost every baker mixes in some wheat to help with the texture; in the Middle Ages loaves with a mixture of rye and wheat where called Maslin loaves. Rye is particularly favored in Germany, and countries to the north and east, although recipes for rye loaves have survived from most marginal regions, such as the Alpine slopes of the Italian Tirol, or the moist maritime province of Galicia in northwestern Spain.

Where rye is appreciated, the sourdough system of bread fermentation is almost universal. This is part science, part history, part taste. Natural sour fermentations (they are called lactic) seem to suit northeastern European tastes—sauerkraut in Germany, sour cream in Russia, and soured or pickled herrings in Scandinavia set the precedent—and rye seems to have an affinity with slightly sharp flavors.

Barley makes an enjoyable bread, but does not have the gluten necessary to make it light like wheat. It is an ancient grain: primitive versions of it have been found on sites in Bulgaria, which yield evidence of the earliest full-scale bakers in Europe. It also can cope with extremes of wet and cold, so it was popular with farmers in lands like Scotland and the far west of Britain. Barley bread is uncommon nowadays.

Another grain that fares well in poor soils and climates is oats, but, like barley, it has mostly disappeared from the modern baker's repertoire. Its principle use was for flatbreads in regions like northern England and Scotland, though it was also an important element in the multigrain breads of Germany, Poland, and European Russia. It has no gluten, so it needs to be mixed with wheat for a risen loaf.

Non-European peoples have converted other grains and staples into breads, or foods that are directly comparable to bread in their role in the society's diet. The maize, or corn, of America is the most obvious example, not only providing the raw material for tortillas and other native breads, but adopted with enthusiasm by European settlers for their Johnnycakes and cornbreads, and exported back to their homelands where the crop grew well in zones not blessed with good wheat: hence polenta of northern Italy, mamaliga of Rumania, and the cornbreads of Spain and Portugal.

An English baker's equipment, at the end of the 19th century

BREAD BAKER'S UTENSILS

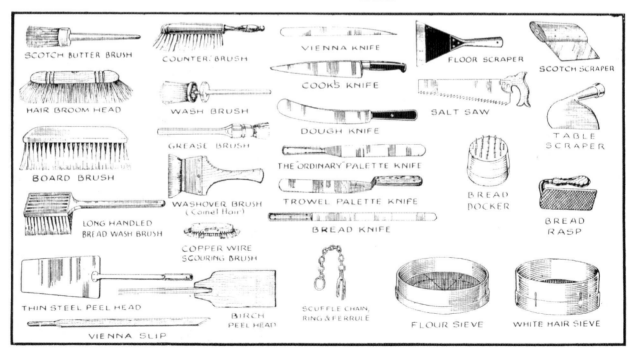

MILLING THE FLOUR

If grains are to be used in cooking, they need to be ground to a flour. Once human numbers expanded beyond the units of a few self-sufficient families, the amount of flour needed to keep everyone from hunger was vastly greater than could be turned out by women at home pounding away in a mortar.

The development of primitive flour-milling involves the shift from the up-and-down crushing of the pestle and mortar to a flat, scraping movement as the bowl of the mortar was opened into a flatter form, and the pestle became a flat stone that was rubbed back and forth across the grain, the flour collecting in a hollow at the end of the base stone.

A to and fro movement was easier work if converted to round and round. If the bottom stone was made slightly conical, and the top stone revolved around its tip, this was faster and less back-breaking. If grooves were cut in the stone, it increased the shearing effect. This simple rotary handmill was the essence of all a mill needed to be.

Such querns, as they are called, were found in the eastern Mediterranean from early classical times; the contribution of the great urban cultures of Greece and Rome was to make these stones, originally operated by two women sitting opposite each other, bigger and faster. Slaves, donkeys, and oxen were made to turn very large mills. Then the brilliant leap was made to using water to drive a wheel, which turned the stones. Water mills meant the stones could be larger and flatter, because the power was so much greater. This brought the possibility of fine flour within the grasp of any community near a mill. Wind power came much later, in about A.D.1000.

Wheat ground between stones was either left as wholewheat (none of the bran extracted) or could be passed through sieves of papyrus, horsehair, or linen of differing fineness to produce flour that was more or less white.

Production of very white flour was made easier when steel roller mills were developed in the 1820s. Multiple rollers ground, or rather pressed the grain, separating the bran, germ, and endosperm. But objections to roller milling exist. It operates too fast, generating heat that damages enzymes in the flour; it creates a characterless and nutritionally inert flour by excluding important components, particularly the germ; and it makes a nonsense of the concept of wholewheat by removing the various components, then adding them back in at the end of the milling process. Stoneground flours are often preferred by people who take their bread seriously.

An emblematic representation of a French baker of the 18th century. Different shapes of loaves, rolls, and pretzels are hung about his person, and he has a baker's peel in one hand, a brush for sweeping the counter and the bottoms of loaves in the other. In the background, one baker is kneading dough in a stone trough, while the other is charging a behive oven—in this case with a separate hearth.

11

LEAVENING AND BAKING

Proving baskets from the beginning of this century. One is for long loaves, the other for rings. French proving baskets are lined with linen; some other baskets are made with fine wicker and need no separate lining, merely thorough dusting with flour.

If a paste is made of flour and water, and cooked right away, the result is a pancake or a lump of dough like the Australian bush food, damper. This could be called bread, but it does not answer most of our requirements of a loaf. This is because it is unleavened.

Some means had to be discovered, in the early days of dough, to fill it with gas and transform it from a tasty morsel to an intricate network of starch and air. That means was fermentation: the natural process of maturation that causes little bubbles of air in a fermenting fluid like beer or wine, or in something even simpler like a paste of flour and water. The discovery of this, too, has been laid at the door of the ancient Egyptians. It probably happened by accident when a batch of dough became infected by the wild yeast spores that float in the air. If, for reasons of economy, the apparently spoiled, sour-tasting, and rotten dough was baked anyway, it would have been realized that the bread was lighter and had a special, good flavor. Later came the thought that a piece of leavened dough could be kept to spread the "infection" to the next batch.

When the Israelites fled from Egypt in the Exodus they left their leaven behind—unlike the more provident prospectors of the American West who carried their cultures with them, hence San Francisco sourdoughs. The Israelites

Fig 19.—Basket for Rising Ring Loaves

thereafter had to exist on unleavened bread. This was the origin of the Passover bread, matzot. But unleavened bread continued to be used in many societies. The Romans, especially in the old-fashioned early days of the Empire, felt that it was traditional, correct, and healthier—the

newfangled leavened doughs were an import from luxurious Greece. Ultimately, the Romans did borrow the use of ale-barm or beermaking yeast from subjected Germanic tribes.

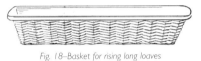

Fig. 18—Basket for rising long loaves

The breads of some societies have relied mainly on lactic fermentation—which is the base of the whole family of sourdoughs—while others, especially in the British Isles, have long depended on straight alcoholic fermentations using beermaking yeast. An inhibiting factor in the adoption of beermaking yeast was its availability: it could not survive extremes of heat, and not all communities had alcohol on the bubble at all times.

EARLY OVENS

The first breads were cooked on flat stones heated directly in the fire. This principle of the griddle or bakestone continues to operate wherever flatbreads like chapatis, bannocks, or tortillas are still the daily diet. It doesn't work, however, if you want to bake: that requires an oven.

It was a natural step to cover the stone with an inverted pot to contain the heat. The domed beehive oven, a freestanding structure with its own source of heat, is the same idea, but on a larger scale. Early examples have been found in Mesopotamia, Egypt, and the Balkans, and it was this concept that spread throughout Europe and the Near East.

The beehive oven is heated by burning a fire on its floor. The flames exit through the door itself or, later, through internal chimneys. When the fire has heated the structure, it is raked out and the risen dough is put in its place. The doorway is sealed, and the bread cooks in a falling heat radiating from every surface, the oven space capturing and recycling any moisture that evaporates from the loaves.

Technical development of ovens did not quicken pace until the 18th century, when improvements in design allowed the more efficient retention, or even introduction, of moisture—hence the crackling thin crusts of Viennese and, eventually, Parisian loaves—and led to methods of remote heating rather than burning fuel on the oven floor.

Since the 19th century, there have been lots of changes in the details of oven design—what it is made from, how it is heated—but the principles have not varied until fairly recently. Now bread moves through ovens on conveyor belts, so that the air alone is heated, not the floor and walls. This is getting very close to steaming the bread, something we in America know only too well, to our regret. It makes for faster production, but not necessarily better tasting bread. However, for the baker trying to provide essential food to a population counted in millions, many of whom are unwilling to pay very much, industrial processes are a necessary evil.

COMMUNAL OVENS

Although ovens can be built any size, there are advantages of time in making them fairly large. The same can be said of mills. Hence bread-baking has often been a communal activity to avoid duplication of expensive resources. Grain was ground at the village mill; dough was baked in an oven owned either by the community, or by a tradesman who gained his living therefrom.

In Greece and the Near East, the village baker cooked bread fashioned in the homes of his customers, as well as baking cuts of meat after the first heat had gone off, just as his fellow bakers in other countries.

PROFESSIONAL BAKERS

The nature of bread production—usually on a larger scale than that of other foods—also gave rise to its early organization as a professional trade. Full-time bakers are identifiable from the records of ancient Egypt, and there are scores of references to them in Athenian comedies. In Rome, there was a bakers' guild from approximately 150 B.C.; in medieval London and Paris, bakers' guilds were among the earliest craft brotherhoods.

A French print of the late 18th century depicting a bakery. On the upper floor is the dough trough and kneading board, as well as sacks of flour; below the oven is being stoked, with wood stored for drying in the cupboard below the oven floor. Buckets, measures, a sieve, a peel, and a scuffle for swabbing out the oven after the fire has been raked out are illustrated at the bottom of the picture.

13

ESSENTIAL TECHNIQUES

Anyone can make a loaf of bread. It is not a difficult art. However, there is great mystery about the magic of yeast and fermentation, and that's not surprising—it is a magical process. At the same time, however, it is a transformation within everyone's grasp.

Most of the skill of baking is about routine and regularity, with a refusal to take short cuts added to the recipe. The ingredients are few in number: just flour, water, salt, and yeast or leaven for most essential breads. These behave in predictable ways, so if you follow the rules, bread will result. Better bread comes from frequent baking.

Imagine the timetable of a professional baker. If there's no bread in the shop by opening time, he won't make a living. If the croissants are not baked before breakfast, when will they ever be eaten? To make sure he keeps to time, he imposes a strict pattern on his work. The dough is mixed to the same recipe; it ferments at the same temperature; the ovens are set at identical heat to yesterday.

He will have to cope with variations—flour may differ from year to year, the weather and humidity will alter the condition of the dough—but he must anticipate these things in order to meet that deadline. As if that were not enough, the baker also has the law to deal with. Each loaf must be the same size, or penalties result. Customers never like to feel cheated. And so the weighing of the pieces of dough works again to a pattern; regularity is key.

The home baker need not worry about weights and measures inspectors, nor even public health regulations, but he or she will do well to follow the same discipline as the tradesman. If you don't know what you have just done, you will never learn by experience and be able to correct your mistakes. Some people keep notes, others rely on good memories. Once you understand it, bread is quite even-tempered: it will accept delays, it will not invariably ruin because you have to run an errand, as long as you don't neglect it, and you know when to stop and devote your whole attention to it.

PREPARING A NATURAL LEAVEN AND YEASTED STARTER

Leavening in bread dough is the extra ingredient that makes a loaf so enjoyable, be it an Ethiopian *injera*, or a large Italian country bread.

Leavening lightens dough by introducing air. If you beat eggs into a cake batter, you incorporate air by the beating action, which the egg white holds and traps by its physical composition. The expanded batter is then set in the heat of the oven. Or you can add chemicals: baking soda, cream of tartar, or baking powder. Here, chemical interaction between substances generates gas for a short time, which can be sealed into the dough by cooking.

FERMENTATION

The way bread is usually lightened is through some sort of fermentation. Fermentation produces gas and heat in many food substances if you leave them for long enough in the atmosphere. Not all fermentation is a good thing: a canning jar that fizzes in the pantry usually needs throwing away, because it is "off;" but some sorts are recognized to do us no harm and to taste nice into the bargain. Milk that ferments turns into yogurt and cheese. Juices and extracts that ferment are transformed into beer, cider, and wine. Vegetables that ferment keep all the winter long (how else could they be stored without freezers) and are served at table as sauerkraut or Korean kimchee.

NATURAL LEAVEN

In a bread dough, flour mixed with water creates a gently sour taste in a lactic fermentation, souring like milk—not alcoholic, turning ultimately to vinegar, which is what happens in a yeast-driven fermentation.

This natural fermentation creates air and generates heat, which further expands the gas. The trick of bread is to mix a fresh dough that can be worked on by a prepared ferment and, lo, a finished loaf! The loaf is conditioned by our working it through mixing and kneading, and it is expanded or raised by the gas of the ferment, and everything is set by the heat of the oven.

Early bakers relied on this spontaneous leaven. It gives a more or less sour taste that often seems to enhance that of the flour. By constant repetition, and keeping the leaven renewed from one day to the next, they built in a degree of reliability. This system is still used by the bakers of France, Germany, and many parts of eastern Europe, as well as Americans making San Francisco sourdough.

YEASTED STARTER

The other important form of leavening is baker's yeast. A natural leaven has wild yeasts in it. They inhabit the air, wherever we turn, and will settle on your ferment and start breeding. Yeast is a fungus that multiplies at enormous speed in the right conditions. Gas and heat are the result of this fast-breeder. Yeasts that just settle are usually wild, weak, and unpredictable: they enhance but do not overpower the spontaneous lactic fermentation of flour and water.

Beermaking yeast, which is a particularly strong form, is a by-product of brewing. Bakers found (as early as the ancient Romans) that using beermaking yeast was a fast way of leavening, and more reliable than a spontaneous fermentation. Some societies have been using it ever since.

I always use fresh compressed yeast as it gives the best flavor and is ready to use immediately. All the recipes in this book use fresh yeast. It is available from bakers, health-food stores, and many supermarkets, and comes as a brown, compressed cake that crumbles easily. It can be stored wrapped in a plastic bag, in the refrigerator up to 2 weeks.

Active dry yeast can be substituted, if preferred. One cake of fresh yeast (0.6 ounce) is equivalent to a $^1/_4$-ounce package (or one tablespoon) of active dry yeast.

Quick-rise dry can also be used. Follow the package directions.

TO MAKE A SOURDOUGH LEAVEN

Natural leavens take a few days to get going. They need to be kept in a warm room and out of drafts. If it is too cold, they will take very much longer to ripen, and then taste too sour. Luckily for us, they keep well in a refrigerator. If you want to start a leaven and use it once a week, you can pinch off a piece of dough, weighing approximately 8 oz (225 g), from the finished dough when you have made it, put it in a glass bowl, cover it with plastic wrap, and store it in the refrigerator. A day or two before you want to bake, take up the recipe below from the point of the second refreshment.

The starter
* *$^1/_2$ cup (60 g) wholewheat flour (wheat or rye depending on the sort of loaf you want)*
* *2 tablespoons spring or filtered water (chlorine in water supplies is best avoided)*

Mix the flour and water to a paste and knead it with your fingers and thumbs until it is a smooth, firm dough.

Put this nut of dough in a glass or small bowl, cover it with cheesecloth (not plastic wrap), and leave it in a warm place, at approximately 75-80°F, for about 2 days.

Although the outside will crust over, the inside will be moist and slightly aerated. The smell will be sweet.

Discard the crust and proceed with the first refreshment.

The first refreshment
* *¹/₄ cup (60ml) spring or filtered water*
* *1 cup (120 g) wholewheat flour*

Dissolve the starter in the water, add the flour, and mix to a dough. Knead with the fingers on a work table.

Put the dough in a small bowl and cover with plastic wrap. Put it back in your warm spot and leave for a day or two. It will crust again, but it will also have enlarged, and the aeration will be greater. The smell will be very slightly sharp.

Discard the crust and proceed with the second refreshment.

The second refreshment
* *¹/₂ cup (120 ml) spring or filtered water*
* *scant 2 cups (225 g) unbleached white bread flour*

Repeat as for the first refreshment, but this time leave it for about 8-12 hours and it should show every sign of life: growing and rising like a normal piece of dough with a slightly sharp edge to the smell, but not rotten or "off."

The leaven is now ready to be added to a dough that will proceed as any other, though often more slowly.

The recipes I have given that use leavens, for instance French Country Bread (see page 30) or the German Sourdough Rye Bread (see page 76), give instructions from almost the very beginning of the process.

TO MAKE A *BIGA* (YEASTED STARTER)

The Italian *biga* is a piece of matured dough with a speck of yeast in it. It gives loaves a more interesting texture than they would get from a simple yeast dough ripened for only a few hours.

* *1¹/₂ cups (60 g) unbleached all-purpose plain flour*
* *¹/₂ cake (7 g) fresh yeast*
* *6 tablespoons (90 ml) tepid water*

Make a well in the middle of the flour, crumble in the yeast, and add the water. Mix to cream the yeast, then extend the mixing to incorporate the flour.

Mix until all the dry flour has been taken up, then knead on a work surface to a stiff and smooth dough. Let rise in a bowl, covered with plastic wrap, overnight (12 hours or more) at a temperature not less than 70°F.

It should rise once and fall back again before being used for a bread dough, as detailed in the recipes for Ciabatta (see page 44), Italian Country Bread (see page 48), and North Italian Rye Bread (see page 51).

Left: *The ingredients for a* **biga** *(yeasted starter) are fresh yeast, flour, and water.*
Right: *Mix the flour, yeast, and liquid until all the dry flour has been taken up.*

MIXING

Mixing the dough happens when you first combine all the weighed and measured ingredients. It sounds very simple, but what is done at this stage will sometimes affect the outcome of your ideal loaf.

Take care to follow the recipe's instructions about starting the mix: sometimes a leaven or starter is dissolved in water; sometimes flour and salt are mixed dry, a well is made in the center, then yeast is crumbled into the well and water is added; sometimes yeast is creamed in water or milk and added as a liquor to the flour.

Sugar used to be a constant ingredient in bread recipes, but modern yeasts do not usually need sugar to help them become active, nor a proofing stage to be sure they are still.

Mixing gets all the dry ingredients evenly wetted. If you are mixing a big batch of dough, this is more difficult than it may seem—the last scraps of flour take a long time to be incorporated. The mixing should, therefore, be done with generous sweeps of the hand (this is usually better than using a spoon), making sure that you get the water to all the corners, so that all the flour is mixed in.

Mix the liquid into the flour with your hand. This is usually better than a spoon when mixing large amounts.

TEMPERATURE OF THE LIQUID

Yeast will die if it is overheated (say above 120°F) and will be slowed or dormant if the temperature is too low. If you add boiling hot water to a dough, you will probably kill the yeast and nothing will rise. If you add stone-cold liquor, then the yeasts will take correspondingly longer to become active— 77°F is their ideal operating temperature.

The temperature of the water will therefore depend on how fast you want the dough to develop. Sourdoughs are more sensitive than baker's yeast. If you keep them too cool, they will move too slowly.

The home baker does not need to worry too much about temperature, though the professional must do so, otherwise his bread will take a variable amount of time to ripen and may miss the first rush of customers. There are some recipes—wholewheat bread, rye sourdough, or Vienna loaves—where temperature matters, whether keeping the dough warm all the time, or keeping it cool.

ADDING FATS AND OTHER INGREDIENTS

The mixing is also the time that fats and other ingredients are added to doughs. Small quantities of hard fat or oil are no problem. Rub butter into the flour at the outset, or add it melted after the water. Add oil with the water. Some fat helps make the crumb more tender, just as will using milk instead of water. But if a lot of fat is to be incorporated, remember that the fat will coat the particles of flour and stop the yeast fungus from getting to the starch sugars, which are its food. A rich bun or brioche recipe, therefore, should give the yeast a period of time alone with the flour before the fat is added. Such doughs are often made in two stages: a sponge of flour, yeast, and water, and the fat added later.

Spices may be added to the dough in various ways. For instance, saffron is added to Cornish Saffron Bread (see page 63) by making an infusion, which is then mixed with the yeast and liquid before being added to the flour. With Russian Black Bread (see page 90) spices are added to the molasses and yeast. In others, such as French Spice Bread (see page 40), spices are added after the flour and honey have been mixed.

Additions of solid ingredients—currants, raisins, olives, or nuts, for example—will usually be made after the dough has been mixed and given a first bout of kneading. A large quantity of fruit or something similar will only get in the way of working the dough.

Some recipes specify that fruit such as raisins should be warmed slightly before they are scattered over the surface of the dough.

DRY DOUGH

If you feel the dough is too dry, it can be a problem adding more water at the end of mixing. Sometimes you can add a bit more moisture by constantly wetting your hands during the first stages of kneading.

Other times, it can be easier to mix a little extra cold water with some flour to make a smooth paste and then mix that into the dough.

Mix the dough with generous sweeps of the hand, getting the water to all the corners, so the dry ingredients are evenly wetted.

KNEADING

Right: Scrape the dough from the mixing bowl and begin by pressing the heel of one hand firmly into the mass.

Opposite: Swivel the ball through one quarter of a turn and press again with the heel of the hand.

Once the dough has been mixed, it must be kneaded. While mixing combines all the ingredients, kneading conditions them. The key to good bread is conditioning the gluten in the wheat flour.

Wheat flour consists mainly of starch, which gives the loaf its bulk, and gluten, a protein that forms long thin strands to support the weight of starch when the dough is kneaded, and trapping tiny balloons of gas in the dough, preventing their escape—without gluten a loaf of bread would not be light.

You can see gluten in its raw state if you form a ball of flour and water and hold it in a strainer under running water. Soon, the starch is washed off leaving a dense white bean of gluten, for all the world like a piece of chewing gum: stretchy, elastic, and enduring.

Kneading activates the gluten, making the strands longer and stronger.

Wheat flour has the most gluten; rye contains less, yet has some natural gums, so remains sticky during kneading and makes a denser loaf. Barley and other grains like corn have little or none and need wheat flour added to them to hold a loaf shape at all.

Kneading should be done on a clean, flat surface, dusted with flour to keep the dough from sticking. Scrape the dough from the mixing bowl and begin by pressing the heel of one hand firmly into the mass. Push through to stretch it, then lift the leading edge back over to make a ball once more.

Swivel the ball through one quarter of a turn, then press again with the heel of the hand, fold, and turn. Repeating these movements rhythmically, watch the untidy mixture of flour and water convert into a supple, lithe cushion of satin-smooth, elastic bread dough.

HOW LONG TO KNEAD

There is no absolute rule about how long to knead or how many turns to give the dough; it depends on feel. Hard flours

require more work: they will stay grainy in texture longer. It is usually thought that 10 minutes of vigorous hand kneading is sufficient. A soft brown flour will probably take only half that time.

KNEADING IN A BOWL

Some doughs are too moist and runny to be worked on the table at all. An enriched dough made with butter and eggs will often be kneaded in a bowl. Other doughs are kneaded in the bowl before being turned onto the work surface.

Working with moist doughs is one of the aspects of baking that separates the seasoned practitioner from beginners: "Oh! this is far too wet," is a cry often heard at first. But if the dough is kneading by a punching action with thumb and fist in the bowl, then stretched like gum before punching again, it is possible to condition the dough sufficiently to bring it onto the table without vast quantities of flour to stop it sticking.

If a dough is moist, work fast, use the scraper to keep the table clean, and keep your hands clean. Rye doughs present another problem because of natural pentosans which make them gluey. Cleanliness helps, as do wet hands.

When the kneaded dough is supple and elastic, shape it into a smooth ball ready for rising.

RISING

Once the dough has been mixed and kneaded, it is ready for the first rise, when the yeast or other leavening agent does its work through fermentation, creating carbon dioxide gas which is trapped in the dough by the elastic web of gluten. By stretching the gluten in this way, it conditions the flour—gives it exercise. The fermentation process also causes various changes to the starches and enzymes in the flour, further conditioning it.

RISING TEMPERATURE

Usually, dough is left to rise in a warm place, such as an airing cupboard, with a temperature of 75-80°F. Warmth is not essential, but it speeds the process. Although a cold fermentation may be no bad thing, drafts are not so good and play havoc with even development, and too much heat starts to cook the bread.

What is essential is that the dough should be kept airtight so a skin does not form on top. The best thing is to place the dough in a clean bowl, with a tight wrap of plastic over the top of the bowl, or press oiled plastic wrap on the dough itself. A damp dish towel placed over the bowl is another way, but not as effective.

LENGTH OF TIME

How long a dough needs to rise depends on how much yeast or leaven is used and the temperature it is kept at. Some are left in the cool overnight, others take under 2 hours. Usually the first rise sees the dough double in size, and occasionally triple. The time in fermentation will have some effect on the taste and texture of a bread. A simple axiom, proved only by exceptions, is that the slower the ripening of a dough, the better the taste. Wheat has a flavor, but it is difficult to capture. Time is the key.

A long fermentation will probably also imply a small quantity of yeast. This, too, is good for flavor—the flour is not overpowered by the taste of yeast—and is very good for a long life to a bread. Highly yeasted breads do not keep long, nor do short process ones unless additives are thrown into the recipe to delay staling. A leaven bread, using a different form of fermentation and wild yeasts plus a scrap of baker's yeast, keeps for several days.

PUNCHING DOWN

Some bread recipes specify that the dough should rest in two or even three stages, and should be "punched down" after each stage, before it is finally shaped or molded.

This process, where you deflate the risen dough with your fist, and fold it over on itself to recommence the process, has the effect of redistributing the gases created by fermentation, of spreading the yeast through new parts of the dough where it can find more food from the flour, and actually redoubling its activity. This helps to ensure an even texture in the bread.

The subsequent rise is usually faster than the first one. A multi-stage rise seems often to make the bread lighter, as if exercise makes the gluten stretch further.

Above: *Place the dough in a bowl, cover it with oiled plastic wrap and let it rise in a warm place, such as an airing cupboard.*

Left: *At the end of the rising time, the dough will have doubled in size.*

23

SHAPING AND FINAL RISING

Once the first rise (or two or three rises, where this is specified) is complete, the dough is returned to the work surface, punched down and divided if making more than one loaf, ready for shaping or molding.

Instructions for shaping individual breads are normally specified in the recipe, but there are some general tips common to most breads.

Do not use too much flour on the work surface at this stage. For one, it will coat the outside of your shape and make it difficult to pinch together to form an undivided whole. For another, this flour has not been conditioned by any kneading, and if it is rolled into a shape, for instance when making a French baguette, it may appear as an unwelcome streak in the finished crumb.

The point of molding is to produce an unblemished crust on the top of the loaf. If you tear the dough, or stretch it by working too fast or roughly (doughs need to rest between bouts of manipulation, or else the gluten will not stretch smoothly), the crust will be unsightly. This is the reason for sometimes quite detailed suggestions on how to make a shape. A well-molded loaf, even in a pan, will rise higher than a badly shaped one.

RISING CONTAINERS

Some breads are cooked in pans or pots, others are placed directly on the oven floor. The first are given their final rise in the containers destined for the oven. Therefore, the shape is placed exactly as it will appear in the finished loaf, i.e. with the joins or creases on the underside.

Loaf pans should usually be warmed before placing a loaf in them, otherwise the chill strikes the outside of the loaf and slows the rising at that point. This is one cause of dense bottoms to pan loaves that are yet fully risen on the top. Pans also need seasoning or greasing, and nonstick pans are a life-saver to the home baker. To grease them, wipe vegetable oil over the surface with a paper towel. Black pans are better than shiny ones. They absorb the heat while shiny metal reflects it; the crusts in black pans will therefore be crisper.

If you wish to bake something like a round loaf or baguette on a baking sheet, you will either have to put the loaf to rise directly on the baking sheet, or let it rise in a special basket lined with floured linen—these come in round or long shapes—then turn it onto the baking sheet just before baking. The advantage of using baskets rather than rising directly on baking sheets is that the dough does not get chilled or skinned on the outside.

If you have an oven where you can bake on the floor—or perhaps you have invested in a baking stone, which you place in a gas or electric oven to replicate a baker's oven floor—then the loaf will need to rise in a special basket, or a floured wicker basket.

If using a rising basket, the loaf must be placed upside down in it to rise. It is then turned onto a baker's peel (a long-handled wooden shovel) to be slashed, before being shot into the oven. You can buy a peel, or you can make one with a broom handle and a piece of thin plywood, or carve one out of a single piece of wood.

KEEPING THE DOUGH WARM

The final rise is the last one before baking. It does not usually take long, though there are some loaves that are left for more than two, even as much as four, hours. Rising should be done in a warm place (80-85°F); away from drafts. It is important that the outside skin should not crust in the air. Bakers put their loaves in steam-laden rising cupboards, but I use pieces of oiled plastic wrap placed directly on the shaped loaf. They are easily removed unless you don't oil them enough, or you leave the loaf too long.

TIMING

It is always difficult to be sure that timing is correct in rising. Do it too little and the loaf will be tight, or else fly away in the oven. Too much, and the whole thing will collapse. Old Russian bakers were advised to rise their white breads in a tub of water. When the shaped loaf rose to the top, it was ready to bake. You can do the same with a lump of dough in a jar of water. Place it next to the loaves you are rising: when it comes to the surface, they too will be ready.

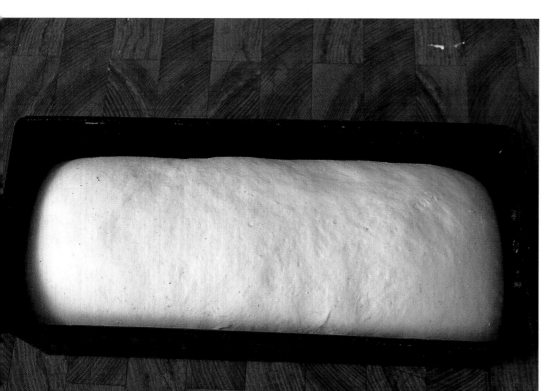

Opposite page: *After the first rise, return the dough to the lightly floured work surface and punch it down before shaping or molding it.*

Above: *The dough is placed in the pan as it will appear in the finished loaf, with the joins or creases on the underside.*

Left: *At the end of the second rising, the shaped dough has almost doubled in size and is puffy in appearance.*

BAKING

The last stage over, the dough has risen, the oven has been heated to the required temperature, and all that needs to be done is to slash the loaves or glaze them before they are baked.

Not every bread is slashed before baking, but many are, and for a practical reason. Even a loaf of perfect rise has a last bit of expansion, called "spring," left in it when exposed to the oven's heat. A loaf that has been underrisen will have lots. Only those that have collapsed through overrising will not rise up again, though a really hot and moist oven will sometimes nearly rescue them.

The heat converts moisture into steam and expands the gases trapped in the dough, while the yeast continues to produce carbon dioxide until it is killed by the heat. The center of a loaf takes a long time to get to the requisite temperature, so rising will carry on until the crust is set (the sugars gelatinized) on the outside and can grow no more.

Slashing or cutting the crust controls the direction, and sometimes the extent, of the spring. Use a serrated knife for slashing the dough—it is easier than a razor, the baker's usual tool. If your loaf is overrisen (does not have much spring), cut it only a little; if underrisen, slash it long and deep. The patterns are not just for visual effect.

MOISTURE IN THE OVEN

Expansion of the crust, and some delay in its setting hard, is also helped by moisture. A baker's oven is completely sealed in a way that a domestic oven is not: moisture evaporating from the loaves is therefore recycled as steam.

However, at home you need to introduce moisture into the oven, either by glazing the loaf (which often helps give the finished loaf a handsome color) or by spraying water into the oven during the first few minutes of the baking time, using a plant atomizer or the thoroughly-cleaned spray attachment from a household cleaner.

Slash the bread with a knife, to control the direction and extent of the spring during cooking.

Some people put a roasting pan in the bottom of the oven and pour boiling water in to create steam during the first part of the cooking time.

Cooking in a baker's oven is done on a falling heat. Start hot and cool down. The first rush of heat maximizes that spring, then sets the crust on it and gives a start to the coloring. So at home the oven will be set at maximum, and loaves baked in the upper half. If bread is baked on two racks, especial care is needed to swap them around to give equal chance of real heat, unless the oven circulates the air.

Major heat may not be needed for all the cooking, and the oven can be turned down for the last half. It is possible that bread baked in pans will have soft crusts in a domestic oven. They can be removed from the pans and finished in the lower heat to crisp the outsides as well as cook the inside.

Cooking removes moisture from the dough, as well as making a hard crust. When testing to see if a loaf is done, the simplest way is to take it in one hand and tap its base with the other. It will sound hollow, and vibrations will travel through the loaf and register on the palm holding the loaf. If not cooked, it will sound utterly dull, with no sympathetic movement. Some loaves are better tested as if they were cakes—insert a fine skewer into the center and see if it comes out dry and clean.

COOLING

Many breads need cooling. This is partly to allow them to continue to evaporate moisture: if you set a cooked loaf directly on the table it would be heavy and moist where it sat. In the old days of country baking, giant loaves, weighing 12-14 pounds, would be cooked once a week. These would take hours and the crust would get thicker and thicker, tougher and tougher. They would be wrapped in a cloth directly they came out of the oven to soften them. The same is done with some flatbreads, but usually cooling is to crisp.

FRENCH BREADS

To some people, France is the home of bread. The baguette or French stick stands in baskets in bakeries the world over, and the heavier, homelier pain de campagne is thought to be the touchstone of hearty goodness.

There are two traditions at work here. Pain de campagne and many of the older breads are made with a leaven or sourdough (though they are never as sour as a German rye bread, for example), while the more modern types, of which the baguette is the most famous, depend on a long fermentation based on yeast.

Yeast was not approved of by French bakers when it first became current among some of their number in the 17th century. It was thought bad for health, and detrimental to a true wheaten flavor, and this opinion has never quite disappeared. So the old way of doing things has never died, even if it has suffered quite a few attacks from industrialization and automation in recent years.

It may be easy to condemn much current French bread as lacking character—simply because everything is done so quickly—but the best of bakers continue to use long fermentation times, whether baking with leaven, yeast, or a combination of the two. It is this leisurely timetable that lets the wheat speak.

Clockwise from center: Pain Polka, French Country Bread, Baguettes, French Rolls, Walnut Bread, and French Hearth Bread.

FRENCH COUNTRY BREAD

Pain de campagne

The method used in this recipe allows you to make two large loaves of sourdough or leaven bread in easy stages over a period of two days. The process is quite lengthy, but it gets around the problem of regular feeding of leaven that often results in lots of bowls dotted around the kitchen. It's all much simpler in a bakery. There, the routine works steadily around the clock. But not everyone wants to bake daily, or indeed needs to.

This recipe, therefore, needs just one preliminary ingredient—a walnut sized piece of leaven, stored in the refrigerator from the last time—then takes you through to finished loaves. If you have no leaven at all, see the instructions for making a leaven on page 16.

When rising the loaf, place a nut of the dough in a jar or measure filled with water at room temperature. When it rises to the surface, the bread is ready to go in the oven.

Makes 2 large loaves

Day 1: 10:00 am
* *walnut of leaven from previous baking*
* *2 tablespoons cold water*
* *$^1/_2$ cup (60 g) unbleached white bread flour*

1 Put the leaven in a bowl and mix with the water, then add the flour and knead to a homogenous dough with your fingertips. Put the dough in a small bowl covered with plastic wrap and let it ripen at about 75°F. It will at least double in size.

Day 1: 5:00 pm
* *7 tablespoons (100 ml) tepid water*
* *the leaven from the previous stage*
* *$1^2/_3$ cups (200 g) unbleached white bread flour*

2 Add the water to the leaven to dissolve it, mix in the flour, and knead the dough on a floured work surface. Let it rise in a bowl, covered with plastic wrap, at about 75°F. It will at least double in size. It will have a definite smell, vinegary and sharp, but not overly strong.

Day 1: 11:00 pm
* *$^3/_4$ cup (175 ml) cold water*
* *the leaven from the previous stage*
* *3 cups (350 g) unbleached white bread flour*

3 Add the water to the leaven to dissolve it, mix in the flour gradually, then knead the dough on a work surface for 10 minutes. Let rise in a bowl covered with plastic wrap at 50°F overnight. It will at least double in size.

Day 2: 8:00 am
* *the leaven from the previous stage*
* *scant 2 cups (450 ml) water at 110°F*
* *5 $^3/_4$ cups (800 g) unbleached all-purpose flour*
* *5 teaspoons (30 g) salt*

4 Make a soup of the leaven and the water, squeezing it between your fingers to break it up. Mix the flour and salt together, then gradually add them to the liquid, mixing the while. Mix to a dough that leaves the sides of the bowl clean, then knead on a floured work surface for 10 minutes, until smooth and resilient. Let the dough rise in a bowl covered with plastic wrap in a warm place (75°F) for between 2 and 3 hours, until doubled in size.

5 Turn the dough onto a lightly floured work surface, punch down, divide in half, and mold each piece into a ball. At this stage, take off a walnut of dough to act as leaven for the next time. Put it in a small bowl covered with plastic wrap, and refrigerate. It will keep undamaged for at least a week, and can then be reactivated for another session of baking.

6 This bread can be risen in *bannetons* (rising baskets) or, with no further molding, on baking sheets. The shape of the *bannetons* will determine whether you have to mold the dough into long loaves or leave them round. Whichever shape, make sure the *bannetons* are well floured, and put the loaves in bottom upward as you will be turning them onto baking sheets, stones, or the floor of the oven itself.

7 Leave for a final rise, covered with oiled plastic wrap to prevent skinning. If you take a nut of the dough and put it into a jar or measure filled with water at room temperature, it will rise to the surface as the yeasts generate gases—just as your loaves are rising in their baskets. When that nut of dough comes to the surface of the water, then your bread is risen and can go into the oven. Rising should take 1-1 $^1\!/_2$ hours. Meanwhile, heat the oven to 450°F.

8 Turn the loaves onto oiled baking sheets, or a baking stone, slash them with a knife (three slashes close together for round loaves, diagonal cuts down the length of longer breads), and bake them for about 35 minutes, spraying them with water three times in the first 5 minutes. If they do not sound hollow after 35 minutes, bake 15 minutes more at 400°F. Cool on wire racks.

BAGUETTES

The "French sticks" that masquerade as baguettes or *bâtards* (the name by which they go in Paris) have for too long made a nonsense of France's great reputation for good bread. Hard and tasteless flours, mechanical processes, and an incredible acceleration of the old-fashioned steady fermentation are largely to blame. What you get nowadays is little more than crust and air, with no flavor and little texture.

It is possible to recreate something of the beauty of this everyday, sometimes twice a day, loaf of city dwellers throughout France in your own kitchen. True, the crackle and thinness of the crust is easier to achieve if you have a purpose-built baker's oven, but the slightly chewy texture of the crumb, and the lightness of the well-risen dough is within the grasp of anyone.

These loaves are made with yeast rather than a leaven, but the fermentation is lengthy to give every chance of developing the flavor, and to reduce the amount of yeast needed to give lift. (Remember, the less yeast, generally the better the taste.) The French call the method *fermentation "sur poolish,"* a reference perhaps to the influence of Viennese and eastern European bakers on Parisian breadmaking during the first half of the 19th century.

If you do not have *bannetons*, you can lay the loaves immediately on a greased baking sheet (crease downward), and let them rise for slightly less time. Or you can buy specially made French baguette molds. Equally, you can make what the French call a *couche*, by flouring a linen cloth and laying each loaf between a fold. Be warned that the knack of extracting the loaves from this arrangement and transferring them to the oven is something learned in time. Disasters are not infrequent.

How the baguettes are baked will determine the character of the crust. Domestic ovens are often not hot enough, nor do they retain enough humidity to give that defined crackle. It is not satisfactory to bake on more than one level—the lower

loaves will not be as good, and changing them around halfway through is not entirely successful. So, if your oven is not large enough to take all the loaves at once you can freeze two of the molded loaves before they have started their final rise. Take them out the next day and carry on from that point.

Makes four 12-inch loaves
* *$2^{1}/_{2}$ cups (300 g) unbleached white bread flour*
* *$2^{1}/_{2}$ cups (600 ml) tepid water*
* *1 cake (15 g) fresh yeast*
* *2 teaspoons salt*
* *$4^{1}/_{4}$ cups (600 g) unbleached all-purpose flour*

1 In a large bowl, mix the white bread flour with 1 3/4 cups (400 ml) of the water, the crumbled yeast, and the salt. Beat well with a wooden spoon. Cover and let rise at room temperature for about 4 hours, until tripled in size. Add the rest of the water, then the all-purpose flour handful by handful, beating with your hand to stretch the gluten. When it comes together into a softish dough, turn it onto a floured work surface and knead for 10 minutes.

2 Let the dough rise in a bowl covered with oiled plastic wrap in a warm place (80°F) for about 2 hours, until at least doubled in size. Return the dough to the lightly floured work surface, divide it into four pieces, and mold them into balls. Let them rest for 5 minutes, crease or join side downward.

3 Take each ball in turn, flip the smooth side underneath, and flatten with the palm of the hand. Fold the right and left sides inward to meet in the center, and press to secure contact. Each ball will now resemble an oblong cushion. Let them rest at the side of the table. These rests are necessary to ensure that you do not tear the dough while shaping it. The more it is worked, the stronger its elasticity. When relaxed, it will form the shape you want very much more easily.

4 Take each cushion in turn and lay it smooth-side down in front of you, the short sides to the right and left. Roll it back toward you, pressing down with your thumbs the whole length of the fold so as to make firm contact. When the first roll is completed, pinch the seam together between finger and thumb. Let rest for 4 or 5 minutes, with the seam on top.

5 Roll these squat sausages to and fro with your fingers splayed out across them. Gently tease more length out of them. Do not press or stretch too much. If you encounter resistance, turn to another loaf. Eventually, you will achieve long loaves of 12 inches, with a smooth side unblemished by crease or tear. Flour your *bannetons* (rising baskets) or grease a baking sheet and place each loaf smooth-side down in the basket or seam-side down on the sheet. Cover the tops with oiled plastic wrap and let rise for a final time at 80°F for about 1 1/2 hours. The tops should not spring back when you press them with a floured fingertip. Meanwhile, heat the oven as hot as possible, at least 450°F.

6 When the rising is complete, turn the loaves out of the *bannetons* onto a greased baking sheet. Slash each of them with a sharp, preferably serrated knife four or five times on a sloping diagonal. The depth of the cut will vary. If they are overrisen (see page 26), shallow cuts will not damage the already delicate structure; if they seem resilient and underrisen, deeper cuts will help the loaf expand in the oven. Put the loaves on the upper rack, and spray them with water immediately, using a plant atomizer or the spray attachment from some household cleaner (scrubbed and purified!). After 2 minutes, spray again, and a third time after 5 minutes. Bake about 20 minutes. The loaves will sound hollow when tapped.

7 If you follow this recipe, each of these loaves will weigh 14 oz (400 g) before going into the oven. When they are cooked, they should lose about 12 percent of their moisture, and will weigh 12 oz (350 g). This is a useful check on whether a loaf is cooked or not. Cool them on wire racks.

Top: When the loaves have risen, turn them out of the bannetons (rising baskets) onto a greased baking sheet.

Bottom: Slash each loaf with a sharp, preferably serrated knife four or five times on a sloping diagonal.

WALNUT BREAD

Pain aux noix

Some people might claim that the most important nut for breadmaking is the chestnut: it was once the staple for many people living in southwestern France, and was itself turned into flour for making a sort of bread. It still is called *le pain de bois*—bread of the woods.

The walnut may never have been turned into a loaf, but it has enhanced many, for its rich and seasoned flavor seems to complement the taste of grains, be they wheat or rye. And walnut bread, sometimes sweetened, as here, with raisins, is a perfect foil for strong cheese.

This wholewheat loaf is enriched with egg and milk, as well as the filling of nuts and dried fruit. The dough should be quite moist because wholewheat has a tendency to dry out. Remember, too, that wholewheat performs best if kept warm through the whole process, from mixing to final rising.

Makes 2 round loaves
* 3 ³/₄ cups (450 g) wholewheat bread flour
* 1 teaspoon salt
* 2 cakes (30 g) fresh yeast
* 1 cup (225 ml) milk at 110°F
* 1 egg
* 1 cup (120 g) chopped walnuts
* 6 tablespoons (60 g) raisins, warmed slightly
* 1 egg mixed with 2 tablespoons milk for glaze

1 In a warmed large mixing bowl, combine the flour and salt. Make a well in the center and crumble the yeast into it. Pour on the warmed milk and mix with your finger to dissolve the yeast and incorporate a little flour. Whisk the egg and add to the liquid. Sweep with your hand around and around the bowl progressively to incorporate all the dry flour, then mix to a dough. When it leaves the sides of the bowl, turn onto a floured work surface and knead for 8 minutes.

2 Flatten the dough on the work surface and scatter the nuts and fruit over the dough. Press them into it with your fingers, then fold the dough up and place in a bowl. Cover with oiled plastic wrap and let rise in a warm place (80°F) for about 1 ¹/₂ hours, until doubled in size.

3 Turn the dough onto a lightly floured work surface, punch down lightly, and divide in half. Gently mold each piece into a ball. Place on warmed, oiled baking sheets and cover with oiled plastic wrap to guard against skinning. Let rise, well out of any drafts, at between 80°F and 85°F. Meanwhile, heat the oven to 425°F.

4 When the loaves are ready (they should no longer spring back when you prod them with a floured finger) brush them both with the glaze and bake for about 35 minutes, exchanging the top loaf for the one at the bottom of the oven halfway through the cooking time. Cool on wire racks.

Top: *French Hearth Bread.*
Bottom: *Walnut Bread.*

FRENCH HEARTH BREAD

Fougasse

Fougasses, which can also be called fouacés, are derived from the same Latin word focus, meaning hearth, as in the Italian focaccia. They are all hearth breads, baked on the floor of the oven just after the fire has been raked out—when its temperature is too high to bake breads without burning the crust. The baker, anxious to test the temperature, tries a little something; the small child, waiting eagerly for the first pull at fresh bread, has a titbit to quell the pangs of anticipation.

To give some character to the flavor, this bread is fermented on a starter of ripened dough from the previous day's breadmaking (it does not have to be fougasse).

Makes 2 loaves
* 8 oz (225 g) of the previous day's dough
* $1/2$ cake (7 g) fresh yeast
* 1 cup (250 ml) tepid water
* $3^{1}/_{2}$ cups (425 g) unbleached white bread flour
* 1 teaspoon salt
* 1 egg mixed with 2 tablespoons milk for glaze

1 Place the previous day's dough in a mixing bowl, crumble in the yeast, and add the water. Squeeze the ripened dough through your fingers to break it up and make a rich soup. Mix the flour with the salt and add to the starter in handfuls, beating vigorously the while. Mix to a dough, then turn onto a floured work surface and knead for 6 minutes. Let the dough rise in a bowl covered with plastic wrap in a warm place (80°F) for about 1 $1/2$ hours, until doubled in size.

2 Turn the dough onto a lightly floured work surface, divide it in half, and mold two balls. Flatten each with the palm of your hand and fold the left and right hand sides to the center, as if folding a business letter in three. Press the crease together with the edge of your hand. The dough should have an oblong cushion shape. Let it rest under oiled plastic wrap for 10 minutes.

3 Using a rolling pin, and with a little flour to stop sticking, roll out the two cushions to rectangles $1/4$ to $1/2$ inch thick and measuring approximately 10 x 6 inches. If the dough resists rolling, do not force it, but rest the piece and turn to rolling the other one.

4 Using the blade of a metal dough scraper, or a pastry cutter, cut four diagonal tears in each rectangle, going almost, but not quite, from edge to edge. Then lay each fougasse on a large oiled baking sheet, stretching and pulling so that it fills the sheet. It need not be immaculately regular—it is meant to seem improvised.

5 Cover the dough with oiled plastic wrap and let rise for about 30-40 minutes. Meanwhile, heat the oven to 450°F.

6 Brush the loaves with the glaze and bake them for about 20 minutes, changing the baking sheets from the top to the bottom rack halfway through the cooking time. When they are cooked, the loaves will sound hollow when tapped. Cool them on a wire rack.

Using the blade of a metal dough scraper, or a pastry cutter, cut four diagonal tears in each rectangle, going almost, but not quite, from edge to edge.

35

FRENCH ROLLS

Pistolets

Professor Calvel, the greatest French teacher of baking in this century, regarded pistolets as one of the finest bread recipes in the war-chest of the journeyman baker. Somehow, it had survived the onslaught of mechanization—which changed so much about French, and every other, bread—and craftsmen were still seen hand rolling the little forms, splitting them with a broom handle, or the edge of the hand, and carefully nurturing them into perfect dinner rolls.

Rolls are the fancy side of baking. They are not usually made with wholewheat or coarse flours, and the wheat has to be the best to give them maximum lightness. They are made with a slightly enriched dough: the extract of malt gives zip to the yeast and a burnished bronze crust, and the milk powder gives tenderness of crumb.

Split each ball of dough nearly in two by pressing down with a smooth piece of wood, such as a wooden spoon handle, nearly to the table.

Makes 16 rolls

* 1¹/₄ cups (300 ml) water
* 1 tablespoon powdered milk
* 1 teaspoon malt extract
* ²/₃ cake (10 g) fresh yeast
* 4 cups (500 g) unbleached white bread flour
* 1 teaspoon salt
* rye or rice flour for dusting

1 Mix the water, milk powder, malt extract, and yeast together. Mix the bread flour with the salt in a bowl and make a well in the center. Pour in the liquid and mix to a dough. Turn onto a floured work surface and knead for 8 minutes. The dough will be moist; make sure that you keep the work surface floured (but not too much) and your hands clean. Let the dough rise in a bowl covered with plastic wrap at room temperature (70°F) for 3 hours. Turn onto the work surface and punch down. Return the dough to the bowl, and let rise once more for about 1 hour.

2 Return the dough to the work surface and divide it into 16 pieces. Roll these into tight little balls by flattening them with your palm onto the table and describing circles with your hand. Gradually lessen the pressure to make a cup of your palm, fingers, and thumb. The dough will turn and lift into a ball. Let these rest under a cloth for 5 minutes.

3 Dust the top of each ball with rye flour or rice flour, then split each of them nearly in two by pressing down with a smooth piece of wood (like a large wooden spoon handle) nearly to the table. Let the dough rest again.

4 Returning to the first roll, pick it up between fingers and thumbs and gently stretch it 1-2 inches along the line of the crease. Repeat for the remaining rolls. Place the rolls on a warmed, oiled baking sheet. Let rise, well covered with oiled plastic wrap, at 80°F, until doubled in size. Meanwhile, heat the oven to 450°F.

5 Bake the rolls on the upper shelf in the oven, spraying water into the oven twice in the first 3 minutes. The rolls should be cooked within 15 minutes. Cool on a wire rack.

PAIN POLKA

This rustic and crusted loaf, so deeply cut before baking that you break off tasty mouthfuls with your fingers rather than cutting tidy slices, is made with a starter of the previous day's dough—in France called simply, *pâte fermentée*. If you are not making bread every day, it will keep longer in the refrigerator. However, the simplest routine is perhaps to make a straightforward bread on one day and keep back enough fresh dough to make a pain polka the next.

Makes 1 large loaf
* 13 oz (375 g) of the previous day's dough
* 1 cake (15 g) fresh yeast
* $1^1/_4$ cups + 2 tablespoons (325 ml) warm water at 80°F
* $5^1/_3$ cups (640 g) unbleached white bread flour
* $2^1/_2$ teaspoons (15 g) salt

1 Put the previous day's dough in a mixing bowl. Crumble in the yeast and add the water. Press the mixture through your fingers until the dough has broken up into a messy soup with a few lumps. Stir in the flour and salt, handful by handful, mixing vigorously with your hand all the while to absorb each addition. Turn the dough onto a floured work surface and knead well for 8 minutes. Let the dough rise in a bowl covered with oiled plastic wrap in a warm place (75°F) for about 2 hours, until doubled in size.

2 Turn the dough onto a lightly floured work surface; at this point remove 13 oz (375 g) of the dough and reserve in the refrigerator for the next pain polka. Punch down the dough and mold it into a single ball. Place it on a warmed, oiled baking sheet, cover the loaf with a piece of oiled plastic wrap, and let rise, out of drafts, at about 80°F for about 1 $^1/_2$ hours, until doubled in size.

3 When you judge the bread ready, heat the oven to 450°F. Dust flour over the top of the loaf, and press gently yet firmly with your hands to flatten it to about two fingers thick. Then score it deeply with a sharp blade, or serrated knife, in a criss-cross pattern, slicing to within $^1/_2$ inch of the bottom. Let it recover for 20 minutes.

4 Bake the loaf for 25-30 minutes, spraying it with water from an atomizer, or something similar, two or three times in the first 5 minutes. Cool on a wire rack.

With a sharp blade, or a serrated knife, score the loaf deeply in a criss-cross pattern, slicing to within $^1/_2$ inch of the bottom.

FRENCH SPICE BREAD

Pain d'épice

All over northern Europe, people once seemed to make celebration gingerbread cookies at the drop of a festive hat. Each town had its own shape, its own recipe, its trademark.

Gingerbread men are still a happy feature on Dutch, German, and British tables, but are not usually seen in France where instead, the spiced bread, pain d'épice, has carried the standard of honeyed sweetness coupled with the bite and zest of spices—always symbols of extravagance and celebration.

It was perhaps a specialty of the north and east of the country; and each city had its own particular set of ingredients and favored combinations.

Some pains d'épice are heavy with chopped candied peel and sliced almonds, but this particular recipe is more even in texture, though the aromas in the kitchen as it cooks are heady and intoxicating.

I have used wholegrain rye flour because the texture seems to gain from a little grittiness.

Makes 1 loaf
* 1 cup (225 ml) honey
* 2¹/4 cups (225 g) wholegrain rye flour
* 2 heaping tablespoons (30 g) granulated sugar
* ¹/2 teaspoon baking powder
* ¹/4 teaspoon baking soda
* ¹/3 cup (30 g) ground almonds
* 2 bulbs stem ginger
* 2 teaspoons fennel seeds
* ¹/2 teaspoon ground cinnamon
* 12 cloves, ground
* grated zest of ¹/2 an orange
* grated zest of ¹/2 a lemon
* a little milk and sugar boiled to a syrup for glaze

1 Warm and melt the honey by standing the jar in a pan of hot water. Measure it, add it to the rye flour in a bowl, and mix together with a wooden spoon. Leave, covered, for 1 hour, for the flour to absorb the liquid.

2 Heat the oven to 350°F. Add the rest of the ingredients, except the glaze, and mix vigorously to be sure everything is spread evenly through the dough. This will be rather sticky; it is the pentosans in the rye flour that always make rye more difficult to handle. Knead the dough on a clean work surface for between 5 and 10 minutes. With rye, it helps if you dip your hands into a bowl of water at intervals during kneading, otherwise you will have a thin coating of gluey rye paste over everything.

3 Press the dough into a well-greased loaf pan that measures about 8¹/2 x 4¹/2 x 2¹/2 inches (or use a nonstick pan). Make sure the dough is pushed right into the corners, using wet hands or the dampened blade of a plastic scraper.

4 Bake the loaf on the middle rack of the oven for about 35 minutes, until a skewer inserted into the center comes out clean. Cracks may open up the top crust, but these are nothing to worry about. When the loaf appears to be done, brush the top of the loaf with the glaze, then return it to the oven for 1-2 minutes to set the glaze.

5 Let the bread stand in the pan for a few minutes, then invert it onto a wire rack. Pain d'épice keeps very well indeed. Because it is made from rye, it improves if it is left a couple of days before cutting into thin slices and buttering for an excellent snack.

Variation: Although rye is the customary grain, it is quite possible to substitute wholewheat flour. In this case, you don't need to wait a couple of days before eating it.

FRENCH SANDWICH BREAD

Pain de mie

Pain de mie—literally crumb-bread, i.e. without crust—was first made to satisfy the demands of tourists from Britain or America who found French loaves too crusty, too rustic, and perhaps too tasty. All that was in the early years of this century. Now the French, too, have been convinced of the utility of this loaf at least for some sandwiches and delicate little canapés. Generally, however, they remain wedded to their baguette.

In the days when bread prices were fixed by government decree and profits were minimal, some bakers begrudged the expensive ingredients such as milk and butter that soften the texture of this loaf and keep it looking white. They used instead grated raw potato.

To keep the crust as thin and soft as possible, this loaf is traditionally cooked in a covered pan, called a pullman loaf pan. Without going to the expense of buying a special pullman pan, simply cover a normal bread pan with an oiled baking sheet and put a stone or other ovenproof weight on the top to hold it down. Alternatively, if you have a cylindrical steamed pudding mold, you can use that.

Makes 1 loaf
* 3 3/4 cups (450 g) unbleached white bread flour
* 1/2 teaspoon salt
* 1 cake (15 g) fresh yeast
* 1/2 teaspoon malt extract
* 1 1/4 cups (300 ml) warm milk
* 2 tablespoons (30 g) butter

1 Mix the flour and salt in a bowl and make a well. Crumble in the yeast and add the malt extract and milk. Shave thin slivers of butter onto the well of liquid. Stir with your finger to dissolve the yeast and then gradually mix in the flour. Mix until the dough leaves the sides of the bowl. Turn onto a floured work surface and knead for 8 minutes. Let the dough rise in a bowl covered with oiled plastic wrap at room temperature (70°F) for about 2 1/2 hours, then punch it down and let it rise again for 1 hour.

2 Turn the dough onto a lightly floured work surface and form a ball. Let it rest, covered with a cloth, for 5 minutes. Flatten the ball with your hands, then roll it into a loaf to fit a long, thin pan (either well-greased or nonstick), measuring about 13 x 4 x 3 1/2 inches.

3 The dough should occupy one-third of the pan. Let it rise, covered with oiled plastic wrap to prevent it from forming a skin, until it has reached three-quarters of the way up the sides. Meanwhile, heat the oven to 425°F.

4 Put the top cover on and bake immediately for about 20 minutes. Remove the cover and continue baking for 15 minutes. Though the crust will not be hard, it should still sound hollow when tapped. Cool on a wire rack.

Note: If the square shape of the bread does not matter to you, this dough makes an excellent fine-textured loaf. Brush the top crust with beaten egg and bake as normal.

Top: *French Sandwich Bread.*
Bottom: *French Spice Bread.*

ITALIAN BREADS

When the world was ruled from Rome, Sicily was the granary of the Empire. "Bread and circuses" kept the people happy, and the emperors made sure it was good wheaten bread, not the barley handed out to slaves and prisoners. Italy's love affair with bread has never ceased, though it faltered in the face of industrialization and mass-produced, characterless loaves. Now, however, regional food is fashionable and breadmaking is restored to its proper place.

One ingredient perhaps best defines Italian bread to the world at large: olive oil. Though it has no part in the thin loaves of big-city bakeries, it enriches and softens the crumb of focaccia and ciabatta—two of the success stories of Italian baking today.

Italian breads are also valued for their rustic simplicity. The open, chewy texture of the pan pugliese, or the denseness of rye bread from the northern mountains near Bolzano, where wheat was not so easy to come by, or the intensity of flavor in olive bread from the groves by the Ligurian Sea near Genoa are proof of the country's breadmaking abilities.

Clockwise from center: *Focaccia, Italian Bread Sticks, North Italian Rye Bread, Tuscan Saltless Bread, Italian Olive Bread Rolls, Italian Country Bread.*

CIABATTA

Italian slipper bread

This dough and the method come from the north of Italy, around the city of Como at the edge of the great Alpine lake, though it has now traveled far from its homeland, and appeals to American and English tastes. The cakey tenderness that comes from olive oil in the dough and the soft yet flavorful crust have won a foreign audience for this Italian loaf.

Ciabatta is not easy to make at home. There are perhaps two things that set trade bakeries apart from home production. The first is the nature of the ovens; the second is the willingness and ability of the professional to handle moist and difficult doughs. Ciabatta is one of the wettest, and the temptation to add more flour is almost irresistible, even though that would change the nature of the loaf itself. The dough is kneaded in the bowl rather than on the table, which helps combat the temptation. Because different flours require different amounts of water, no recipe can get the ratio exactly right.

The flour I use every day is a stoneground organic unbleached white flour of breadmaking quality. It absorbs less water than a finely roller-milled North American hard spring wheat, but rather more than a flour suitable for general kitchen purposes.

A ciabatta made according to this recipe may have better flavor than a commercial loaf inasmuch as it uses the Italian yeasted starter, *biga*, which is ripened for 12 hours or more, to add flavor.

You can also control the quality of olive oil in the dough by finding something fresh and fruity to give that added pungency, though this recipe does not rely on oil to the extent of some other interpretations of the recipe.

Pour the risen dough over the center of the prepared baking sheet. Tease the dough into an oblong about 12 x 6 inches. Use the edge of a dough scraper to push around the edges, or well-floured fingertips to push and tuck the edge.

Makes 1 loaf

* *8 oz (225 g)* biga *(see recipe, page 17)*
* *1 cake (15 g) fresh yeast*
* *$^7/_8$ cup (200 ml) warm water*
* *$2^1/_2$ cups (300 g) unbleached white bread flour*
* *1 teaspoon salt*
* *2 teaspoons powdered milk*
* *1 tablespoon extra virgin olive oil*

1 Put the *biga* in a large bowl and crumble in the yeast. Pour in the water and mix to a soup, squeezing the dough through your fingers to break it up. Mix the flour with the salt and the milk powder, then add to the liquid in the bowl handful by handful, mixing vigorously all the while.

2 When you have added all the flour, pour in the olive oil and continue mixing with circular sweeps of the cupped hand, lifting the dough and stretching it at each beat. Without using a machine, you are conditioning the flour and stretching the gluten. Although it will continue to be impossibly wet, while you work it the flour is absorbing the moisture and taking on more of the character of a normal dough.

3 Eventually change the movement to something more like kneading—bringing the hand around in a sweeping motion, then punching the fist right into the dough. Count on performing at least 1,000 mixing or kneading movements. Pause occasionally, to wipe your brow.

4 Let the dough rise in a bowl, covered with plastic wrap, in a warm place (80°F) for about 2 1/2 hours. It will grow considerably.

5 Warm a baking sheet with and dust it heavily with flour. Pour the risen dough onto the center of the baking sheet, then work this rough pile into an oblong shape measuring about 12 x 6 inches. Either use the edge of a dough scraper to push around the edges, or well-floured fingertips to push and tuck the edge into shape.

6 Shake flour over the top of the loaf, cover it with oiled plastic wrap and let it rise at 80°F for about 45 minutes. It will spread as well as rise. Meanwhile, heat the oven to 450°F.

7 Bake the bread in the center of the oven for 20-25 minutes. Cool on a wire rack.

FOCACCIA

Italian hearth bread

Although pizza may be the best-loved product of the Italian baker's oven, it could soon be challenged by the focaccia. Both are hearth breads, originally cooked on the oven floor before the chief event of the day, the baking of the really big loaves. The French version of focaccia, fougasse, is given on page 35.

Focaccia was the baker's hors d'oeuvre. As soon as the fire had been raked out, he popped these inside the door to cook quickly while the temperature of the oven settled and the hot-spots on the roof died down, so that the large loaves, which would be left in for an hour or more, would not be irretrievably burned. (Burned bread is almost a thing of the past today, but it happened as regular as clockwork in the old ovens. Grandfathers will remember that their parents would often ask the baker for an outside loaf—one that had been cooked right at the edge of the oven, where the heat was at its most fierce and the crust was correspondingly dark.)

Makes 2 loaves

* 2 cakes (30 g) fresh yeast
* 1 cup + 3 tablespoons warm water
* $^1/_4$ cup (60 ml) white wine
* 5 cups (600 g) unbleached white bread flour
* 2 teaspoons salt
* 2 tablespoons extra virgin olive oil
* sea salt crystals and extra virgin olive oil for the topping

Dimple the focaccia with the fingertips of one hand, pressing nearly to the bottom of the loaf.

1 Cream the yeast in the water and the wine. In a large bowl, mix the flour with the salt and make a well in the center. Pour in the liquid and mix to a dough. Mix vigorously until it comes away clean from the sides of the bowl. Add the olive oil and mix to incorporate.

2 Turn the dough onto a floured work surface and knead for 10 minutes. The dough will be moist, so keep your hands clean and use a dough scraper to assist in the handling. Use as little dusting flour as possible while working the

dough. Let the dough rise in a bowl, covered with oiled plastic wrap, in a warm place (80°F) for 1-1 $^1/_2$ hours, until at least doubled in size.

3 Turn onto a lightly floured work surface, divide in half, and mold into two balls. Pat each of them flat and extend them with palms and fingers to disks about 10 inches in diameter. If they resist your stretching, let them rest for a few minutes under a sheet of oiled plastic wrap. Put them on two well-greased pizza pans.

4 Cover the disks with oiled plastic wrap and let them rise in a warm place (80°F) for 30 minutes. Remove the plastic wrap and dimple the focaccia with your fingertips, pressing nearly to the bottom of the loaf. Replace the plastic wrap and let the dough recover for up to 2 hours. Meanwhile, heat the oven to 450°F.

5 Scatter crystals of sea salt over the surface of the loaves and drizzle oil into the dimples. Bake for about 20-25 minutes, spraying water into the oven with an atomizer three times in the first 5 minutes. If you have to put the pans on different racks in the oven, swap them from top to bottom halfway through the cooking time. Cool on wire racks.

ITALIAN COUNTRY BREAD

Pan pugliese

This flavorful country bread comes from the heel of Italy, Apulia. It gets tenderness from olive oil, lots of taste from the *biga*, and a deep crust into the bargain. Traditionally, it was risen in the farmhouse in a cloth-lined basket, taken to the village bakehouse, turned onto a baker's peel, and slipped onto the floor of the oven. The same technique can be followed at home, but maneuvering this soft loaf onto a peel and slipping it onto a sheet or stone already in the oven is a tricky procedure, and many will find it safer to turn it carefully out of the basket onto a warmed and oiled baking sheet. Alternatively, it can be risen directly on the baking sheet. It will spread quite alarmingly, and the final rise will be more subject to drafts and patchy cooling, but the end result is still scrumptious.

Punch down the dough on a lightly floured work surface, then shape it into a ball.

Makes 1 large loaf
* 7 oz (200 g) biga (see recipe, page 17)
* 1¹/₄ cups (300 ml) tepid water
* 1 cake (15 g) fresh yeast
* 2 teaspoons salt
* 2 tablespoons olive oil
* 4 cups (500 g) wheatmeal (85% extraction) bread flour; or equal parts unbleached white and wholewheat (100%) bread flour

1 Combine the *biga*, water, yeast, and salt in a bowl; mix to dissolve the *biga* by squeezing it through the fingers of one hand. Add the olive oil, then add the flour a handful at a time, beating all the while. Mix to a dough that has some resilience, then turn it onto a floured work surface to knead. It will be quite moist, but will come together with working as the flour absorbs all the liquid. Knead for 10 minutes. Let the dough rise in a bowl, covered with oiled plastic wrap, in a warm place (75°F) for about 2 hours, until nearly tripled in size.

2 Turn the dough onto a lightly floured work surface, punch down, and shape into a ball. Let it rise upside down in a floured, cloth-lined rising basket, or the right way up directly on an oiled and warmed baking sheet. Let the dough rise, covered by oiled plastic wrap, for 1-1 ¹/₂ hours, until doubled. Meanwhile, heat the oven to 450°F and put a deep, empty baking tray or roasting pan in the bottom. If you are rising the loaf in a basket, place a baking sheet in the oven.

3 Dust the loaf lightly with flour and score with a checkerboard of slashes, or leave it to crack freestyle in the oven. Place it in the oven and pour a little water into the baking tray or roasting pan. Turn your loaf from the basket onto a baker's peel, then slide it onto the warm baking sheet, or simply place the loaf that has risen on the baking sheet into the oven.

4 Bake the loaf on an upper rack for 30-40 minutes. If your the crust browns too quickly, turn the oven down to 425°F after 20 minutes. The loaf is cooked when it sounds hollow when tapped. Cool on a wire rack.

ITALIAN OLIVE BREAD

Olive bread has become quite fashionable in countries far away from the olive belt. Perhaps it's because the flavor captures those hot Mediterranean evenings.

Makes 1 loaf or 6 rolls

* 3 cups (350 g) unbleached white bread flour
* $^1/_2$ teaspoon salt
* 1 cake (15 g) fresh yeast
* $^2/_3$ cup (150 ml) tepid water
* 2 tablespoons olive oil
* $1^1/_4$ cups (175 g) olives (black, or a mixture of black and green)

Left: Italian Olive Bread Rolls.
Right: North Italian Rye

1 In a bowl, mix the flour and the salt together, make a well in the center, and crumble in the fresh yeast. Pour the water over the yeast and stir with your finger until it is creamy. Add the olive oil, and extend your stirring in scope and force to incorporate the flour. Mix vigorously, eventually kneading the dough by bringing the hand around in a sweeping motion, then plunging the thumb through the dough with a sharp punch. Do this about 100 times, then let the dough rest, covered, for 15 minutes.

2 Meanwhile, pit and chop the olives. Scatter them over the dough and knead in the bowl to mix them in. Turn the dough onto the work table and knead conventionally to ensure that the olives are evenly distributed. Let the dough rise in a bowl covered with oiled plastic wrap in a warm place (75°F) for 1 $^1/_2$ hours, until doubled in size.

3 Turn the dough onto a lightly floured work surface, punch down lightly and mold into a single loaf—either a ball or an oval—or individual rolls. To make an oval, flatten the dough into a round, fold it in half away from you, to make a half-moon, and press the two halves together. Start rolling it toward you from the center, pinching the join with the heel of your hands as you make each turn. When the roll is completed, pinch the crease between finger and thumb. Tidy the points by gently rolling the loaf on the table with the palms of your hands. Transfer to a warmed, oiled baking sheet.

4 Cover with oiled plastic wrap and let rise at 80°F for about 1 $^1/_2$ hours. Meanwhile, heat the oven to 425°F. Brush the bread with olive oil and make three diagonal slashes on the top if making a loaf. Bake a loaf for 35-40 minutes, rolls for about 15 minutes. Cool on a wire rack.

NORTH ITALIAN RYE BREAD

In the mountains of northern Italy, wheat is as difficult to grow as it is in other European highlands, and breads of other grains have been a staple for centuries. Rye bread is the most important, and in districts that fall under the Austrian and German spheres of influence, for instance the Tirol, the baking of rye bread is a direct link to the larger Central European tradition.

I first learned of this rye and wheaten bread in Carol Field's intelligent book about Italian baking, *The Italian Baker*. It is yeast-based, rather than a sourdough, and uses the gluten of wheat flour to make a lighter loaf. It is made with the Italian yeast starter, *biga*, which has a particularly good flavor due to its long fermentation time.

Makes 1 large loaf

* 6 oz (175 g) biga (see recipe, page 17)
* 1 cake (15 g) fresh yeast
* 1 1/2 cups (350 ml) warm water
* 4 1/2 cups (450 g) wholemeal rye flour
* 1 1/2 cups (225 g) unbleached all-purpose flour
* 1 tablespoon salt
* 2 teaspoons crushed caraway seeds

1 Put the *biga* in a bowl and crumble in the yeast. Add the water and mix to a soup by squeezing the *biga* through your fingers.

2 Mix the flours, salt, and caraway seeds and add them to the liquid gradually, mixing all the while. Mix to a dough, then turn onto a floured work surface and knead for 10 minutes. Add more water if the dough seems too stiff, or knead it while repeatedly wetting your hands in a bowl of warm water. The rye will make the dough sticky, so keep your hands and work surface clean.

3 Let the dough rise in a bowl, covered with oiled plastic wrap, in a warm place (85°F) for about 2 hours, until doubled in size.

4 Turn the dough onto a lightly floured work surface. Punch down and mold into a ball. Flatten the ball to a disk under the weight of your hand, then fold the right and left sides in to meet at the center. Roll this cushion shape into a long roll, pinching the join between finger and thumb.

5 Put this roll into a floured rising basket, seam uppermost, for the final rise, or place it seam downward on a greased and warmed baking sheet. Cover with oiled plastic wrap and let rise in a warm place (85°F) for 1-1 1/2 hours. Meanwhile, heat the oven to 450°F. If using a rising basket, place a baking sheet in the oven to preheat.

6 Make four or five holes down the center of the loaf with a skewer to enable the loaf to expand. If you have risen the loaf in a basket, turn your loaf onto a baker's peel, then slide it onto the preheated baking sheet and make the holes.

7 Bake for 20 minutes, spraying water onto the loaf three times in the first 5 minutes. Then reduce the heat to 400°F and bake for another 20-30 minutes, until the loaf sounds hollow when tapped. Cool on a wire rack.

TUSCAN SALTLESS BREAD

One of the paradoxes in recipes for this deservedly popular bread is that many of them suggest adding a pinch of salt to make it more palatable. Bread without any salt is strangely mute, though when this commodity was hard to come by or heavily taxed, it was often omitted by bakers. The French once used to think English bread impossibly salty, the high seasoning masking the natural nuttiness of the flour.

Salt does have a useful function, particularly in yeasted breads. Although salt may attack yeasts and even kill them if used to excess, it also conditions the flour, making it firmer and more resilient, while yeast in a way makes flour softer and less textured.

To make the starter, pour the boiling water onto the flour and mix to a batter. Leave overnight.

The saltless bread of Tuscany circumvents the problem of flavor by serving as a natural accompaniment to salty foods like cured hams, salamis, or anchovies. Its open texture and rustic character ensures that it looks the part as well as tastes it.

Makes 1 loaf

Starter (to be made a day ahead)
* $^7/_8$ cup (200 ml) boiling water
* 1 cup (120 g) unbleached white bread flour

Dough
* $^3/_4$ cup (175 ml) warm water
* 1 cake (15 g) fresh yeast
* $3^3/_4$ cups (450 g) unbleached white bread flour

1 To make the starter, pour the boiling water onto the flour and mix to a batter. Leave uncovered overnight.

2 The next day, add the warm water to the starter and crumble in the yeast. Mix to a soup. Add the flour and mix or knead in the bowl to form a slack dough. Knead carefully for 5 minutes, keeping your hands as clean as possible. Let the dough rise in the bowl, covered with oiled plastic wrap, in a warm place (80°F) until doubled in size.

3 Turn onto a well-floured work surface and lightly fold the dough into a ball. Place the ball with the crease or joins uppermost on a 12-inch square, shallow baking pan, liberally sprinkled with flour. Cover with oiled plastic wrap and leave to rise again until doubled in size.

4 Have ready a similar baking pan, oiled and slightly warmed. Place it carefully on the top of the risen loaf so that the shape is somewhat flattened then flip pans and dough over so the smooth and floury side of the dough faces upward. Let it recover for 20 minutes. Meanwhile, heat the oven to 425°F.

5 Slash the top of the loaf with a sharp serrated knife, or leave it to crack freestyle in the oven. Bake for about 35 minutes, until golden. Cool on a wire rack.

ITALIAN BREAD STICKS

Grissini

Homemade grissini put any manufactured ones to shame. For one thing, they have taste. Eating them reminds us what good playthings they are for the hands and mouth before a meal: "They make so pleasant a noise between the teeth," was the comment of one 19th-century novelist on discovering them in Piedmont, their original north Italian home.

Makes 15 sticks
* 1 cake (15 g) fresh yeast
* 1 cup (250 ml) tepid water
* 3³/₄ cups (450 g) unbleached white bread flour
* 2 teaspoons salt
* 3 tablespoons olive oil
* sesame seeds or poppy seeds for topping (optional)

1 Cream the yeast in the water. In a large bowl, mix the flour with the salt. Make a well in the center and pour in the yeast mixture, then the olive oil. Mix to bring the dough together, then turn onto a floured work surface and knead for about 10 minutes. The dough will be soft.

2 Shape the dough into an oblong cushion or rectangle of about 12 x 4 inches. Cover with oiled plastic wrap and let rise in a warm place (85°F) for about 1 1/2 hours, until doubled in size. Meanwhile, heat the oven to 400°F.

3 When the dough is fully risen, leave it plain, or brush lightly with water and sprinkle generously with sesame or poppy seeds. Cut the oblong shape crosswise into three sections, then cut one section into five parts and lift and stretch each piece until it becomes a stick. They will not need rolling—the dough is soft enough to stretch virtually under its own weight. Lay the sticks on a slightly warmed and greased baking sheet. Repeat with the remaining two pieces of dough.

4 Bake for 15-20 minutes, changing the baking sheets from top to bottom halfway through the cooking time if you have had to use more than one. Cool on a wire rack.

Variation: The action of the dough can be accelerated by the addition of a teaspoon of malt extract at the first mix. This dough makes an excellent, light pan loaf, tender to the tongue, with the crispest of thin crusts. Don't cut the dough into breadsticks, but mold it for a pan, let rise for 40 minutes, then brush the top with beaten egg and milk to glaze, and bake in a hot oven (425°F).

Above: Lift and stretch each piece of the dough until it becomes a stick. Lay the sticks on a warmed and greased baking sheet.

BRITISH BREADS

There is more to British bread than sometimes appears. Not all is factory produced, bland, and spongy. Just as it seemed as if the British were to lose their bread traditions, people began to appreciate that different recipes and more complex procedures could produce bread worth eating again. Valuable lessons have been drawn from bakers around the world that methods need to change as well as appearance.

Britain has favored yeast as the powerhouse of its bread for many centuries—perhaps due to the British love of beer. Sourdough leavens have existed, but not survived. In earlier times, care was taken to keep the amount of yeast to a minimum, and work to long fermentation times, which enhanced the flavor of fairly straightforward doughs. But this, too, has largely gone by the board in favor of highly yeasted short-process breads.

What struck foreign visitors to Britain most forcibly in historical times was the affection for white bread shared by all sections of the population, rich or poor. Though highland regions might have been forced to eat rye, barley, or oats cooked on a griddle rather than in ovens, most of the population ate fine (or not so fine) white loaves. It is a modern paradox that brown flour, despised for centuries, has become a premium food in the search for better health.

Clockwise from center: English Wholemeal Bread, Harvest Loaf, Saffron Bread, Cottage Loaf, Barley Bannock, Split Pan Loaves, and Soda Bread.

BARLEY BANNOCK

Bannock is a generic description of flat breads cooked in Scotland, Ireland, and the north of England—i.e. those regions where wheat was not the primary staple grain. The grain used in bannocks might differ, just as it does in loaves of bread, but the common factor was that they were cooked on a griddle and were unleavened.

They are quite delicious—not as enriched as girdle or drop scones, certainly not as sweet, but they make a wonderful tea bread nonetheless. In this recipe, the bannock is cut into sections before being cooked. Strictly speaking, once they are cut, they are scones, though common usage would now define scones as sweetened and containing currants.

Makes 1 round, cut into 4

* *1 cup + 3 tablespoons (120 g) barley flour*
* *7 tablespoons (60 g) unbleached all-purpose flour*
* *$^1/_2$ teaspoon cream of tartar*
* *$^1/_2$ teaspoon salt*
* *$^2/_3$ cup (150 ml) buttermilk, or if buttermilk is unavailable milk and plain yogurt mixed half and half*
* *$^1/_2$ teaspoon baking soda*

Above: Form the dough into a ball and press it with your hand to form a disk about 1/2 inch thick. Cut the disk into four.

Right: Cook the bannock sections on a preheated griddle for 4-5 minutes on each side until brown.

1 Sift the flours, cream of tartar, and salt together into a bowl. Mix the buttermilk and yogurt with the baking soda and add to the bowl. Bring together into a soft dough; work it briefly on a floured work surface. Form the dough into a ball and press it with your hand to form a disk about $^1/_2$ inch thick. Cut the disk into four equal triangles.

2 Heat a griddle on top of the stove (if you don't own a griddle, use a heavy skillet). It should be hot but not burning—when you hold your hand about 1 inch above the surface it should warm the palm.

3 Cook the bannock sections for 4-5 minutes on each side until brown. Wrap them in a cloth to keep the outsides soft, and eat them quite soon after cooking.

SPLIT PAN LOAF

Although many British loaves, especially in the last 30 years, have become simple doughs that take no more than an hour or two to make, there are more lengthy processes that still find favor particularly because they allow time for the wheaty taste to develop, and for as little yeast as possible to be used which is both economical and good for long-keeping.

One of these methods is called the Scottish sponge, due to the runny sponge, made the night before, which acts as a ferment for the whole dough. This recipe is made according to the same system. The loaves are baked together in a block, though not in the same pan. You will find that packing them close together in the oven encourages high rising, and sometimes a wild movement toward each other.

Makes 4 loaves

The first sponge
* 3 3/4 cups (450 g) unbleached white bread flour
* 1 teaspoon salt
* 1/2 cake (7 g) fresh yeast
* 1 cup (250 ml) cold water

Second stage
* 3 3/4 cups (800 ml) tepid water
* 1/4 cake (4 g) fresh yeast
* 5 cups (700 g) unbleached all-purpose flour
* 2 1/2 teaspoons salt

Final dough
* 5 3/4 cups (800 g) unbleached all-purpose flour
* 2 tablespoons (37 g) salt
* 1/4 cup (60 ml) tepid water

1 Mix the flour and salt for the first sponge in a medium-sized bowl. Make a well in the center and crumble in the 1/2 cake of yeast. Pour the cold water over the yeast and stir with your finger to dissolve. Draw in the flour and mix thoroughly. Turn the dough onto a floured work surface and knead for 10 minutes, until entirely smooth. It will be firm. Let the dough rise in a bowl covered with oiled plastic wrap at room temperature overnight.

2 The next day, break the ball of risen sponge into small pieces in a bowl large enough to hold the final dough. Pour on the tepid water for the second stage and mix to a slurry, squeezing it through your fingers. Crumble the 1/4 cake of yeast into this thick soup, then add the second stage flour and salt, mixing vigorously. At this stage the dough will be very moist and impossible to knead. Give it at least 200 beats with your hand, or a large mixing spoon, to condition the flour. Leave the bowl, covered with oiled plastic wrap, in a warm spot for about 1 hour, until doubled in size.

3 Mix together the flour and salt for the final dough, then mix it gradually into the sponge. When all of it has been added, draw in the last bits of dry flour with a little tepid water. Mix until the dough pulls away from the sides of the bowl. Turn onto a floured work surface and knead for 10 minutes. The dough will be supple, but not too wet.

4 Let the dough rise in a bowl, covered with oiled plastic wrap, in a warm place for about 1 1/2 hours, until doubled in size. Turn onto a lightly floured work surface, divide into four pieces, and form them into balls. Roll into shape and place in four warmed and greased loaf pans measuring about 8 1/2 x 4 1/2 x 2 1/2 inches. Cover with oiled plastic wrap and let rise in a warm place until domed above the tops of the pans. Meanwhile, heat the oven to 450°F.

5 Cut the loaves with a sharp knife down the length of the top to give a "split pan" shape, if desired. Bake the loaves close together at the top of the oven for 15-20 minutes, then reduce the oven temperature to 400°F and bake for 20 more minutes. Cool the loaves on wire racks.

ENGLISH WHOLEMEAL BREAD

The English were once a nation of white bread enthusiasts. Foreign visitors remarked how even the poorest classes afforded white bread, made from flour bleached by dubious methods. Brown bread, as in ancient Rome, was thought to be the diet only of failures and criminals. This changed upon the discoveries of the benefits of bran, and the lack of texture and flavor in much mass-produced white bread.

Makes 2 loaves

* 6$^1/_2$ cups (800 g) stoneground wholewheat bread flour
* 2$^1/_2$ teaspoons salt
* 1$^1/_2$ cakes (25 g) fresh yeast
* 2 cups (475 ml) warm water (100°F)
* $^1/_4$ cup (60 ml) vegetable oil

1 Preheat the oven to its minimum temperature. Warm the mixing bowl under hot running water, put in the flour and salt, and place in the oven until evenly warmed. Make a well in the middle and crumble the yeast into it. Pour in a third of the water and stir with a finger. Leave for 3 minutes, then add the rest of the water and the vegetable oil.

2 Mix the flour into the liquid. Continue to mix until you have a shaggy mass with the flour evenly wetted. Turn the dough onto a floured work surface and knead until it comes away cleanly from the surface and shows considerable elasticity—this can take anything from 8-15 minutes. Replace the dough in the bowl. Cover it with oiled plastic wrap and let it rise in a warm place (80°F) until doubled in size.

3 Turn the dough onto a lightly floured work surface and punch it down. Divide into two pieces and shape each gently into a ball. Let rest for 3 minutes while you warm and grease two loaf pans that measure 8$^1/_2$ x 4$^1/_2$ x 2$^1/_2$ inches or one large loaf pan that measures 12 x 5 $^1/_2$ x 4 inches. Shape the loaves by flattening them lightly and rolling each into a stubby sausage, then put them into the pans. If using one large pan, mold the loaves as two balls and place them next to each other. They will part easily when baked. Cover with oiled plastic wrap and let rise in a warm place (80°F) until they rise to the top of the pans. Meanwhile, heat the oven to 450°F.

4 Place the bread on an upper middle rack and bake for 15 minutes, spraying the oven with water twice in the first 5 minutes. Then reduce the oven temperature to 400°F and bake for 15 minutes more. Test the loaves to see if they are cooked: they will sound hollow when tapped. If the crust is not sufficiently crisp when the loaves are cooked, return them to the oven, without their pans, for another 10 minutes. Cool on wire racks.

Top: *English Wholemeal Bread*
Bottom: *Saffron Bread*

SAFFRON BREAD

This recipe is commonly associated with the county of Cornwall in England, but it was not always so. The crocuses whose stamens yield saffron were cultivated throughout southern England, just as they were in continental Europe and further afield. Medieval cooks loved the golden color, as well as the heady flavor. By the Victorian period, however, Cornwall and the southwest were particular English strongholds of the taste. They called it "cake" rather than bread, but it was cooked as bread or buns.

Makes 2 loaves

Saffron infusion
* 1 envelope (1 g) saffron stamens
* 6 tablespoons (90 ml) water
* $^1/_2$ teaspoon granulated sugar

First stage
* the saffron infusion
* $^7/_8$ cup (200 ml) tepid milk
* $^1/_2$ teaspoon granulated sugar
* $1^1/_2$ cakes (25 g) fresh yeast
* $^1/_2$ cup (60 g) unbleached white bread flour

Second stage
* $3^1/_2$ cups (400 g) unbleached white bread flour
* $^1/_2$ teaspoon salt
* 5 tablespoons (60 g) granulated sugar
* 4 tablespoons (60 g) butter
* 1 extra large egg
* 1 teaspoon lemon juice
* the ferment made in the first stage
* 1 cup (120 g) golden raisins, slightly warmed

Glaze
* 5 tablespoons (60 g) granulated sugar
* 2 tablespoons (30 ml) water
* squeeze of lemon juice

1 To make the saffron infusion, empty the saffron into the water in a pan and bring to a boil. Add the sugar and simmer for 30 minutes. Bring to a boil again, then cool to tepid. Mix the saffron infusion with the tepid milk and the $^1/_2$ teaspoon sugar. Crumble in the yeast and stir in the flour for the first stage. Let ferment for 30 minutes.

2 Put the flour, salt, and sugar for the second stage in a bowl and cut in the butter. Mix the egg and lemon juice into the ferment. Make a well in the center of the flour and pour in the ferment. Mix to a dough. Turn onto a floured work surface and knead for 5 minutes. The dough will be soft, but try to work it with as little additional flour as possible. Let it rest for 15 minutes. Add the warmed raisins and knead again to incorporate them evenly. Return the dough to the mixing bowl, cover tightly with oiled plastic wrap, and leave it to rise in a warm place (80°F) for at least 1 $^1/_2$ hours.

3 Grease two slightly warmed loaf pans measuring $8^1/_2$ x $4^1/_2$ x $2^1/_2$ inches. Turn the dough onto a lightly floured work surface, punch down lightly, and divide in half. Mold two loaves to fit the pans, cover them with oiled plastic wrap, and let rise in a warm place for about 45 minutes. They should rise to fill the pans. Meanwhile, heat the oven to 425°F.

4 Bake the loaves in the center of the oven for about 25 minutes. The crust will at first be soft, but they should still sound hollow and feel light when handled. Meanwhile, make the glaze: put the sugar, water, and lemon juice in a pan and bring to a boil. Brush the cooked loaves with the glaze and let cool on wire racks.

Note: This bread dries out quite quickly and is best eaten fresh, though it can be toasted. It is also possible to shape the dough as buns (to make 12-16). You can make hot crossed or any other bun by omitting the saffron and varying the fruit.

COTTAGE LOAF

Place the smaller ball on top of the larger, making sure you position it in the center, then carefully press a hole through the center from top to bottom, using the first three fingers and thumb of one hand held in a cone shape.

The cottage loaf is perhaps the ultimate symbol of British traditional baking. Yet this shape is one of the most difficult to get right. The dough needs be firm so that the bottom half does not collapse under the weight of the top. The joining of the two needs to be firm yet gentle. All too often, the "hat" topples off. If it does the bread will be none the worse for being misshapen.

Makes 1 loaf
* *2 cups (300 g) unbleached all-purpose flour*
* *1¹/₄ cups (150 g) unbleached white bread flour*
* *2 teaspoons salt*
* *1¹/₂ cakes (25 g) fresh yeast*
* *⁷/₈ cup (200 ml) warm water (80°F)*
* *2 teaspoons vegetable oil*
* *beaten egg for glaze*

1 Sift the flours and salt into a bowl and make a well in the center. Crumble the yeast into the well and pour on the water. Stir with your finger to dissolve the yeast. Add the oil and mix to a dough. When it pulls away from the sides of the bowl, turn it onto a floured work surface and knead for 10 minutes. The dough will be firm.

2 Let the dough rise in a bowl covered with oiled plastic wrap in a warm place (80°F) for 1 ¹/₂ hours, until doubled in size. Turn onto a lightly floured work surface, punch down, and form two balls, the first made of one-third of the dough, and the second made of two-thirds. Divide by weight if you are unsure. Let them rest for 5 minutes, covered with oiled plastic wrap.

3 Gently flatten the top of the larger ball and the bottom of the smaller one. Moisten the bottom surface of the smaller one with a brush dipped in water. Place the smaller ball on top of the larger, making sure you position it in the center, then carefully press a hole through the center from top to bottom, using the first three fingers and thumb of one hand held in an approximate cone shape.

4 Place the loaf on a floured baking sheet and brush with the beaten egg. Cover with oiled plastic wrap as well as a large glass bowl inverted over the loaf, to prevent a skin forming on the outside of the dough. Let recover and rise in a warm place (80°F) for about 40 minutes. Meanwhile, heat the oven to 400°F.

5 When risen, brush again with beaten egg, then use scissors to snip small cuts at 2-inch intervals around the outsides of both the top and bottom sections of the loaf. These will help the expansion of the loaf in the oven.

6 Bake the loaf in the bottom of the oven, preferably under a "bonnet" of a large saucepan or metal bowl inverted over the loaf (allowing plenty of room for growth). This will equalize the pull of the oven and encourage the loaf to rise straight, as well as keeping the crust soft and expandable for as long as possible. Bake for 20 minutes, then remove the "bonnet" and bake for 15 minutes more so that the crust can brown. Cool on a wire rack.

HARVEST LOAF

Bread has always been turned to purposes other than mere sustenance. Just as it is itself a symbol of survival and nourishment, so particular shapes are used to add further layers of meaning: the braided strands of the Jewish challah recall the Temple breads, Greek loaves are made in the form of a dove at Eastertide, and so on. In England, the most famous modeled loaf is without doubt the harvest sheaf, displayed in churches for the Harvest festival. Its apparently complex form is a simple matter of construction, and its message is unambiguous.

Any number of shapes can be constructed out of bread. If they are dried out very slowly (in a gas oven on pilot light, for instance), they can be preserved without deterioration for a matter of years. It is best if the dough is made stiff, and the loaf should not be underrisen when it is put in the oven, otherwise it runs the risk of rising too much during the baking, thus distorting the chosen form.

Using a sharp knife, cut out a mushroom shape (with a large head and a short stem) to fit on a greased baking sheet or an upturned baking tray.

Makes 1 loaf
* $6^1/_2$ cups (800 g) unbleached white bread flour
* $2^1/_2$ teaspoons salt
* 1 cake (15 g) fresh yeast
* $1^3/_4$ cups (400 ml) cold water
* 1 egg mixed with 2 tablespoons milk for glaze

1 Mix the flour and salt in a bowl. Make a well in the center and crumble in the yeast. Add the water and mix with your fingers to cream the yeast. Mix in the flour to make a dough. When it pulls away from the sides of the bowl, turn it onto a floured work surface and knead thoroughly for at least 12 minutes, until the dough is smooth. Let the dough rise in a bowl, covered with oiled plastic wrap, in a warm place (75°F) for 1 ¹/₂ hours, or until doubled in size. Turn onto the work surface, punch down, and form into a ball. Cover with oiled plastic wrap and let rest for 5 minutes.

2 Flatten the ball with the palm of your hand, fold the right and left sides in to meet in the center, and press the seam together with the heel of your hand. The dough should be shaped like an oblong cushion. Flour the work surface and roll out the dough to a rectangle approximately ¹/₂ inch thick. It may need to rest for 5 minutes during this rolling, to avoid tearing. Cover it with a cloth if it does need to rest, to prevent a skin from forming.

3 Use a sharp knife to cut out a mushroom shape (with a large head and short stem) to fit on a greased baking sheet or the bottom of a baking tray 18 x 12 inches. Lift this shape onto the greased sheet or tray and prick it all over with a fork. This is the base of the wheatsheaf. Brush it with cold water to prevent a skin from forming.

4 Divide the remaining dough into two pieces, one twice
the size of the other. Reserve the smaller portion under
oiled plastic wrap. Divide the larger piece into five equal
sections, then divide each of those into 16 pieces. You should
have 80 tiny pieces of dough. Working quite quickly, roll each
of these between the palms of your hands to make tapered
sausages, i.e. the ears of corn. Use a pair of sharp scissors to
snip each ear three times down the center, and once on either
side, as in the illustration below.

5 As you make them, press the ears of corn onto the top half
of the base, arranging first a row lapping over the top
edge, then a second row overlapping the gaps between those
in the first, and so on until the top half of the sheaf is filled. If
the base shows signs of drying out, brush it again with water.

6 The remaining small piece of dough should be rolled out
to a length about equivalent to the stem of the wheatsheaf
base and cut into 20 or 30 thin strips. Lightly roll and stretch
these to fit the base to represent stems. Build up toward the
center to give the stems depth. Braid the last three strips and
place the seam where stems and ears meet.

7 Brush the whole loaf with the glaze. Let it rise in a draft
free place, with a sheet of oiled plastic wrap lightly over
the top. Watch it carefully to be sure it does not overrise; if it
is put into the oven too soon, it will expand wildly, opening
up surface cracks. Meanwhile, heat the oven to 425°F.

8 Brush the loaf with glaze again just before putting it in the
oven. Bake for about 20 minutes, then reduce the
temperature to 375°F and bake for 20 minutes more. When
cooked, it will sound hollow when tapped on the base. As long
as you glazed it carefully, the crust will be a uniform gold.
Cool on a wire rack.

Note: If your oven cannot take this size of wheatsheaf, reduce
it to fit, baking any left-over dough as a conventional loaf.

*Above left: Divide the larger piece of dough from the trimmings into five sections,
then divide each of these into 16 pieces. Roll each of these between the palms of
your hands to make tapered sausages, i.e. the ears of corn. Use a pair of sharp
scissors to snip each ear three times down the center and once on either side.*

*Above: Roll out the remaining small piece of dough to make 20-30 thin strips. Affix
them to the base to represent stems, building up toward the center to give depth.*

SCOTTISH BAPS

The bap is a Scottish "morning goods", sold by bakers in time for breakfast, elevenses, or lunch. The bun is light as air, and the crust yieldingly soft.

Scottish baps are at their best eaten warm, straight from the oven, but they can be reheated very successfully—either warm them in a mild oven or split them and toast them under the broiler.

Baps also make the ideal packed lunch.

Makes 8
* 2 cakes (30 g) fresh yeast
* 1$^1/_2$ cups (350 ml) tepid milk and water mixed in equal quantities
* 3$^1/_4$ cups (450 g) all-purpose flour
* 2 teaspoons salt
* extra flour for dusting

1 Cream the yeast in the warm milk and water. Sift the flour together with the salt into a large bowl and make a well in the center. Pour the yeast liquid into the well and mix to form a slack dough.

2 Knead lightly in the bowl, then cover with oiled plastic wrap, and let rise in a warm place for about 1 hour, until doubled in size.

3 Turn onto a lightly floured work surface and divide into eight portions. Knead these into balls, cover, and put aside for a few minutes.

4 Using a floured rolling pin, gently roll the dough balls into 4-inch rounds. Try to make sure that you roll right to the edge of each round so that no air remains trapped there.

5 Lay the rounds out on a greased and floured baking sheet, giving them space to rise and expand. Cover with oiled plastic wrap and let them rise in a warm place for about 30 minutes, until well risen. Meanwhile, heat the oven to 425°F.

6 Brush the tops of the baps with milk, then dust generously with flour (Scottish baps are traditionally floury, rather than glazed). Press a floured finger into the center of each one to equalize the air bubbles and prevent any blistering on the top when they are baked.

7 Bake the baps for 15 minutes, until lightly browned. Dust them with more flour as soon as they come out of the oven and then let them cool on a wire rack. They should be eaten as soon as possible.

Pour the yeast liquid into the well in the flour and mix to form a slack dough.

BARLEY BREAD

The ancient Greeks once thought barley was the prince of grains, though by the time of Imperial Rome it was more often the diet of slaves, and in general it falls far behind wheat and rye as the raw material of bread. One problem is that it has no gluten to provide lift and elasticity, so it will make a heavy loaf unless it is combined with another grain. In the highlands of Britain and Europe, where wheat does not grow easily, barley has nonetheless held an honorable position in the bakehouse, and its use has sometimes spread beyond the uplands when wet summers have occasioned poor wheat harvests. Some old bread recipes combine both barley and potatoes for an acceptable loaf, but the recipe given here uses barley and wheat flours.

Top: Barley Bread
Bottom: Soda Bread

Makes 1 small loaf
* 1 cake (15 g) fresh yeast
* 1 cup (225 ml) warm water
* 2 tablespoons heavy cream
* $1^{1}/_{2}$ cups (175 g) stoneground wheatmeal (85% extraction) flour, or equal parts unbleached all-purpose flour and wholewheat (100%) flour
* $1^{3}/_{4}$ cups (175 g) barley flour
* 1 teaspoon salt
* a little egg white mixed with 1 teaspoon of cold water for glaze

1 Cream the yeast in the warm water and heavy cream. Mix the flours and salt in a bowl and make a well in the center. Pour the yeast liquid into the well and mix to form a dough. Turn onto a floured work surface and knead for 8 minutes.

2 Let the dough rise in a bowl, covered with oiled plastic wrap, in a warm place (75°F) for about 1 $^{1}/_{2}$ hours, until doubled in size. Turn onto a lightly floured work surface, punch down and mold into a ball. Flatten the ball with the palm of your hand and carefully roll up to form a simple loaf

to fit a slightly warmed and greased loaf pan that measures $7^{1}/_{2}$ x $3^{1}/_{2}$ x $2^{1}/_{4}$ inches. Try not to tear the surface of the roll when shaping it. Cover with oiled plastic wrap and let rise in a warm place (at least 75°F) for 1 hour. Meanwhile, heat the oven to 425°F.

3 Brush the loaf with the egg white and water glaze, and bake in the center of the oven for about 25 minutes. The loaf is cooked when it sounds hollow when tapped. Let it cool on a wire rack.

SODA BREAD

While many soda breads are made with wholewheat flour, a white loaf is a handsome addition to the tea table.

This kind of bread was once universal in Ireland—its special appeal was perhaps its economy of fuel and its adaptability to cooking on an open hearth rather than in an elaborate baker's oven. Like other traditional Irish breads, it did not use yeast, but baking soda and cream of tartar as leavening agents. The normal method of baking was in a covered pot in the embers of the fire. The cook would increase the all-around heat by heaping coals on the lid. My suggestion of a "bonnet" in the oven imitates this arrangement.

If you prefer to make this bread with wholewheat flour, which is perhaps more authentic, it would be best to find a stoneground flour, and ideally as fresh as possible. You may need more liquid in the recipe.

Buttermilk may be difficult to find. It is possible to substitute milk and water with some cream of tartar, or you can use plain live yogurt.

Makes 1 loaf
* $1^1/_2$ cups (225 g) unbleached all-purpose flour
* $^1/_4$ teaspoon baking soda
* $^1/_4$ teaspoon cream of tartar
* $^1/_4$ teaspoon salt
* 1 tablespoon (15 g) butter
* 4 teaspoons (15 g) granulated sugar
* $^2/_3$ cup (150 ml) buttermilk or half milk, and half water plus $^1/_4$ teaspoon cream of tartar)
* 1 medium egg

1 Sift the flour, baking soda, cream of tartar, and salt together into a bowl. Cut in the butter and sugar. Mix the buttermilk, or milk and water, with the egg and add to the flour. Mix lightly, then turn onto a floured work surface. The dough should be quite moist.

2 With clean and floured hands, bring this softly into an approximate round. It will not be smooth and neat, and it is best if you do not work the flour too much. Making a firm, kneaded dough excites the gluten in the flour, making the dough tough and heavy. Heat the oven to 350°F.

3 Use a knife to mark a cross from one side to the other and place the loaf on a greased baking sheet. Cover this with a "bonnet"—a bowl or saucepan that is larger than the loaf—which will equalize the heat in the oven and give maximum lightness while not browning the crust too much. Bake for 30 minutes, then remove the bowl or saucepan and bake the loaf for 15 minutes more, until lightly browned.

4 Soda bread is best eaten warm and fresh. When cooling it on a rack after baking, wrap it in a clean dish towel to keep the crust soft.

Remove the pan or saucepan for the last 15 minutes of the baking time to brown the loaf lightly.

EUROPEAN BREADS

In northern and eastern Europe, rye is the predominant grain in breadmaking, with wheat falling second. The strong, sour flavors of the foods of Germany and eastern Europe complement the taste of rye perfectly.

The current preoccupation with French and Italian baking should not be at the expense of the immense variety of breads available from Germany, Scandinavia, or Austria, as well as other Eastern European and Balkan countries. Sometimes they are dismissed as "pumpernickels," but the Austrians are perhaps the finest pâtissiers in Europe, and it was the combination of Viennese knowhow and strong Hungarian wheat that gave us the most common European bread form, the French stick.

In parts of Europe where weather was more extreme and the conditions of life more difficult, the breads reflected the peasants' preoccupation with survival. Only in towns and cities did people expect to buy bread everyday; in country districts the oven might be fired only once a month. Hence many recipes were for breads that could be dried, or kept a long time without spoiling.

Clockwise from center: *Vienna Bread, Portuguese Combread, Russian Black Bread, Finnish Easter Bread, Swedish Flat Rye Bread, Pretzels, Austrian Gugelhupf.*

PORTUGUESE CORNBREAD

Broa

Although corn is not native to Europe, it was adopted with great enthusiasm by many communities when it was introduced by the explorers of the New World. Often it reached them by circuitous routes and became known by such names as "Turkey corn," since it seemed to come from the east, not the west.

Corn was especially valuable in regions where wheat was not the grain of first recourse—where, for instance, rye and barley, or rice, had been adopted for reasons of climate or agricultural preference. Thus it is often found on the margins: the northeastern corner of Italy, or in northern Portugal and Galicia, the region of northwestern Spain around Santiago de Compostela where the country is washed by Atlantic rain.

Broa is from northern Portugal, where the Galicians make a cornmeal and barley bread. This broa is a hearty loaf to be eaten with soups and stews and other strong-tasting foods. It can be made with finely ground cornmeal, or use a coarse grind if you desire a crunchier texture. Although some recipes for cornbread suggest making a porridge of cornmeal and water before combining it with yeast and wheat flour, this method is more direct.

Right: Portuguese Corn Bread

Makes 1 giant loaf
* *2¹/₂ cups (300 g) yellow cornmeal*
* *2 teaspoons salt*
* *1¹/₂ cakes (25 g) fresh yeast*
* *³/₄ cup (175 ml) tepid milk*
* *1¹/₄ cup (300 ml) tepid water*
* *2 tablespoons olive oil*
* *4¹/₂ cups (600 g) unbleached all-purpose flour*

1 Mix the cornmeal with the salt. Cream the yeast in the milk and water and add to the cornmeal. Add the olive oil. Beat in the flour gradually to form a pliable dough.

2 Turn the dough onto a floured work surface and knead it for 5 minutes. Let it rise in a bowl, covered with oiled plastic wrap, in a warm place (80°F) for about 1 ¹/₂ hours, until doubled in size.

3 Turn onto a lightly floured work surface and punch down vigorously. Form it into a large ball.

4 Place the ball seam-side down on an oiled baking sheet. Cover the dough with oiled plastic wrap and let it rise in a warm place for about 1 hour, until it has doubled in size. Meanwhile, heat the oven to 375°F.

5 Bake the loaf for 35-45 minutes, until uniformly brown and hollow sounding when tapped on the base. Cool on a wire rack.

MAJORCAN POTATO BUNS

Coca de patatas

Elizabeth Carter describes in her book, *Majorcan Food and Cookery,* how these light buns for morning coffee or teatime are often made with the pulp of orange- or yellow-fleshed sweet potatoes (yams), but may also be prepared with ordinary white potatoes.

Makes 8
* *8 oz (225 g) potatoes*
* *1 cake (15 g) fresh yeast*
* *²/₃ cup (150 ml) tepid milk*
* *scant 2 cups (225 g) unbleached white bread flour*
* *²/₃ cup (120 g) granulated sugar*
* *2 tablespoons (30 g) lard*
* *1 extra large egg*

1 Bake the potatoes in their skins until soft, then peel them, discarding the skins. Mash the pulp with a fork.

2 Cream the yeast in the tepid milk. Mix the flour and potato pulp in a bowl with the sugar. Cut in the lard.

3 Make a well in the center and add the yeast liquid. Add the egg and mix to form a dough. Adjust the texture by adding more milk or flour—potatoes vary in their absorption of liquid. The dough should be moist but not unworkable.

4 Turn the dough onto a floured work surface and knead for 5 minutes.

Turn the dough onto a floured work surface and knead for 5 minutes.

5 Let the dough rise in a bowl, covered with oiled plastic wrap, in a warm place (75°F) for about 1 hour, until doubled in size.

6 Turn the dough onto a lightly floured work surface and divide it into eight pieces. Shape these into round balls and place them well apart on a greased baking sheet. Cover with oiled plastic wrap and let rise for 30 minutes, until they have doubled in size. Meanwhile, heat the oven to 200°F.

7 Bake for about 15 minutes, until the buns are nicely browned. Cool on a wire rack.

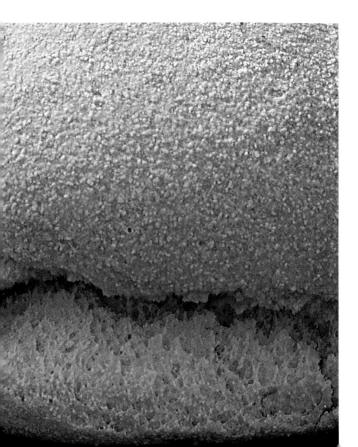

GERMAN SOURDOUGH RYE BREAD

This is a combination bread, using the rising-power of two forms of fermentation: lactic, from the spontaneous fermentation of flour and water with help from wild yeasts—this gives the sour flavor; and alcoholic, from the compressed yeast that we use every day to raise conventional yeasted doughs.

Sourness complements the flavor of rye—one reason for using a sour culture when making rye breads. Rye does not have as much gluten as wheat, hence it is often combined with wheat to make a lighter loaf. There are certain pentosans in rye that make it seem sticky or gluey when being worked. One solution is to knead the dough with wet hands. The cleaner you keep your hands and work surface, the easier kneading will be.

The natural composition of rye flour also means that rye bread is best when it is a day or two old. If you slice it too fresh, the knife glues up and drags across the cut surface. Do not expect rye to make a very airy, light loaf—slices should be as thin as possible to enhance the bread's tenderness.

I have always followed the advice of my friend, Rolf Peter Weichhold, who grinds his own flour in a windmill built on the medieval town walls of Xanten in northern Germany, and bakes his bread in an oven deep in the fortifications below: start from scratch with this recipe. There is no need to carry over starters or ferments from one batch to the next, although you can set up a routine to do this if you want. This is a three-day recipe, starting from scratch.

Makes 2 large loaves

Days 1-2: the starter
* 9 tablespoons (60 g) stoneground wholegrain rye flour
* $^1/_4$ cup (60 ml) warm water at 110°F
* pinch of caraway seeds

Day 3, 9:00 am: the leaven
* $1^1/_4$ cups (300 ml) warm water at 110°F
* 2 tablespoons of the starter
* 3 cups (300 g) stoneground wholegrain rye flour

Day 3, 5:00 pm: the dough
* 4 cups (500g) finely ground wholewheat flour
* 3 cups (300 g) stoneground wholegrain rye flour, plus extra rye flour or rye flakes for rolling
* 1 cake (15 g) fresh yeast
* $1^3/_4$ cups (400 ml) warm water at 110°F
* 2 teaspoons salt
* the ripe leaven

1 To make the starter, mix the rye flour and the warm water in a bowl, add the caraway seeds, and knead with your fingertips to make a dough. Place it in a glass jar and cover with a piece of waxed paper. Leave it in a warm place (80°F) for 2 days, stirring with a teaspoon twice a day. As it begins to ferment, it will rise and form a domed top, then the top will flatten, and sink to leave a shallow crater. It is ripe when the top is risen, but flat. It can be refrigerated at this point, and will hold for several days.

The dough for this bread is molded into two balls and rolled in rye flour or rye flakes before being placed in the pan.

2 On day 3 in the morning, prepare the leaven. Mix the warm water and 2 tablespoons of the starter to a soup. Add the flour handful by handful, mixing all the while. Leave it in a bowl covered with a cloth for about 8 hours, at about 85°F. When it is ripe, it should taste pleasantly sour.

3 After 8 hours, make the dough. Warm a mixing bowl and warm the flours. Cream the yeast in a small amount of the warm water. Mix the flours and the salt and make a well in the center, then add the leaven, the creamed yeast, and most of the remaining water. Mix to a dough, cover, and leave for 10 minutes in a warm spot. Mix again, adding the last of the water, if necessary. The dough should not be too wet. Turn it onto a floured work surface and knead for at least 10 minutes.

4 Let the dough rise in a bowl, covered with plastic wrap, in a warm place (85°F) for about 1 $^1/_2$ hours, until nearly doubled in size.

5 Turn onto a lightly floured work surface, punch down and divide in two. Mold the pieces into balls. Grease one loaf pan measuring about $8^1/_2$ x $4^1/_2$ x $2^1/_2$ inches or two loaf pans measuring about $7^1/_2$ x $3^1/_2$ x $2^1/_4$ inches. If using a large pan, the balls may be put in as they are, after moistening the tops and rolling them in rye flour or flakes. Place them adjacent to each other in the pan. If using smaller loaf pans, flatten the balls on the work surface, fold the right and left sides of the circle to meet at the center, turn the shape around so that the long edge faces you, and roll toward you, pinching the seam with the heel of hand and thumb as you roll. Moisten the top and roll in rye flour or flakes.

6 Cover the pans with oiled plastic wrap and let rise for 30-45 minutes. Meanwhile, heat the oven to 450°F.

7 If baking in the large pan, bake the bread on an upper rack for 20 minutes, spraying the loaves with water three times in the first 5 minutes. Reduce the oven temperature to 400°F and bake for another 20 minutes, then reduce the temperature to 350°F and bake for a final 20 minutes. If using the smaller pans, reduce each 20 minute period to 15 minutes. The loaves are cooked when they sound hollow when tapped. Cool on a wire rack.

PUMPERNICKEL

Pumpernickel originated in Westphalia, on the banks of the Rhine. It is a dark and dense rye bread, cooked extremely slowly, which has no apparent leavening, though it does ferment spontaneously during its long rest in the pan before baking. It is steamed rather than baked, and the slow cooking ensures that it keeps very well. Breads that cook fast never keep long, and the giant loaves that were once baked over a matter of hours in a cooling oven would keep for a number of days, if not weeks. Pumpernickel, which keeps for months, served as a form of insurance against the day when the grain ran out and no more bread was available—a realistic possibility when peasants' lives were turned upside down by invasion, pestilence, or famine. It was also a way of using leftovers from the mill, because the best flour for this bread is a really coarse grind, almost a meal. Nowadays, however, it is valued for its intense flavor, a natural foil to foods like smoked hams or strong cheese.

When the cooking is finished, cool the bread on a rack, and delay slicing the loaf for a day or two, then cut it into the thinnest slices possible.

At the beginning of the fermentation time, the dough will come halfway up the pan (see right). By the end of the rising time it will reach the top of the pan.

Makes 2 loaves, or 1 large loaf

* 5 cups (1.2 litres) pints water at 147°F
* 1 tablespoon salt
* $^1/_2$ teaspoon each of ground aniseed, coriander, fennel, and caraway
* 6 cups (600 g) wholegrain rye flour, coarsely ground
* $3^3/_4$ cups (450 g) wholewheat flour, coarsely ground
* $2^1/_4$ cups (225 g) barley flour
* scant 1 tablespoon (15 g) honey (not heat-treated)

1 Mix all the ingredients, except the honey, in a bowl. Add the honey and mix to form a dough. Divide between two nonstick baking pans, measuring 8 $^1/_2$ x 4 $^1/_2$ x 2 $^1/_2$ inches, or use one larger pan, measuring 12 x 5 $^1/_2$ x 4 inches.

2 Press the moist dough into the corners and flatten the top with a wet metal spatula. Cover the pan(s) loosely with oiled plastic wrap and leave in a warm place (85°F) for 16-20 hours. There will be a spontaneous fermentation and the bread will rise in the pan. It will also smell quite unusual, but do not be discouraged by this.

3 Heat the oven to 225°F. Place a roasting pan of boiling water in the oven and place a rack on the pan. Cover the

baking pans tightly with foil, place them on the rack, and bake for 5-6 hours. The loaf should feel firm. Increase the oven temperature to 350°F, remove the foil, and bake for 30-60 minutes more, to make the top crusty.

4 Leave the bread in the pans for a few minutes, after which the loaves should come out easily. Cool completely on a wire rack. Store the loaves wrapped in plastic wrap or foil.

PRETZELS

There are two sorts of pretzel (called *brezeln* in German). One is a hard and salty biscuit that helps sharpen the thirst for a long, cool drink of beer; the other is a larger and softer salted bread sold especially in America, having been brought over by German immigrants in the 19th century.

The name refers to the shape, which is very ancient—made by early Christians as a Lenten bread, the crossed arms symbolize the cross. The name derives from the Latin *bracellae*, "little arms." Both breads and cookies are made to this pattern in Germany and Austria.

The pretzel is like a bagel in that it is poached before baking, giving it a chewy texture.

Roll each piece of dough into a pencil, then bend into a horseshoe. Bring the ends up to the top of the shoe, crossing and twisting once in the center.

Makes 16

* 1 cake (15 g) fresh yeast
* $^7/_8$ cup (200 ml) tepid water
* 6 tablespoons (90 ml) tepid milk
* 3 $^3/_4$ cups (450 g) unbleached white bread flour
* 1 teaspoon salt
* 2 tablespoons (30 g) butter, melted
* 1 egg beaten with 2 tablespoons milk for glaze
* sea salt crystals

1 Cream the yeast with the water and milk in a bowl. In a separate bowl, combine the flour and 1 teaspoon salt. Make a well in the center of the flour and pour in the liquid. Mix to a rough dough, adding the melted butter while mixing. Mix thoroughly until the dough pulls away from the sides of the bowl. Turn onto a well-floured work surface and knead for 5 minutes.

2 Let the dough rise in a bowl, covered with oiled plastic wrap, in a warm place (75°F) for about 1 hour, until doubled in size.

3 Turn the dough onto a lightly floured work surface and knead for another 5 minutes. Divide the dough into 16 pieces. Form them into small balls and leave them covered on the side of the work surface.

4 Using plenty of flour to avoid sticking, roll each piece with the flat of your hands into a "pencil" about 12 inches in length. Bend each piece into a horseshoe, then bring the ends to the top of the shoe, crossing and twisting once in the center. Let rise on a floured board, covered with a cloth, for 10 minutes.

5 Heat a large pan of salted water to a bare simmer. Drop each pretzel in turn into the poaching water and remove with a slotted spoon as soon as it rises to the surface. Drain them on a clean dish towel. Meanwhile, heat the oven to 400°F.

6 Place the poached pretzels on greased baking sheets, brush with the glaze, and sprinkle them with sea salt crystals. Bake the pretzels for 25-30 minutes, until golden brown. Cool on wire racks.

SWISS BRAIDED LOAF

Zopf

People in Switzerland, southern Germany, and Austria have a lengthy tradition of fancy baking for feast days, holidays, or just for Sundays. This braided bread, ideal with butter and jam for tea or breakfast, but also good for luxury sandwiches (it contains no sugar), is eaten by Swiss families on Sundays. It is always home-baked because Sunday is the baker's day off. The braid represents the braided hair of the warrior's widow, which she cuts off before joining him in the afterlife.

Top: To make the braid, press the four long pieces together at one end, giving them a little twist and tuck for neatness.

Bottom: Counting from your left, fold 1 over 2, 3 over 1, 4 under 1, and 4 over 3. Repeat until you reach the end.

Makes 1 loaf
* 5 cups (600 g) unbleached white bread flour
* 2 teaspoons salt
* 2 cakes (30 g) fresh yeast
* ²/₃ cup (150 ml) each milk and sour cream, warmed together to 90°F
* 1 egg, beaten
* ¹/₂ cup (120 g) butter, softened
* 1 egg, beaten, for glaze

1 Mix the flour and salt in a bowl and make a well in the center. Crumble the yeast into the well and add the warm milk and sour cream. Mix to dissolve with your fingers. Add the beaten egg and the butter, and mix to form a dough. Turn onto a floured work surface and knead for 5-10 minutes, until soft and shiny. Let the dough rise in a bowl, covered with oiled plastic wrap, in a warm place for about 1 hour, until doubled in size.

2 Turn the dough onto a lightly floured work surface, punch down and form into a ball. Divide this into four pieces and roll each piece into a sausage shape about 10 inches long and 1 inch thick. You may have to work in stages, with a little rest in between, so as not to stretch the dough too quickly.

3 To make the dough into a braid, press the four long pieces together at one end, giving them a little twist and tuck for neatness.

4 Counting from your left, fold strand 1 over strand 2, 3 over 1, 4 under 1, and 4 over 3. Repeat until you reach the end. As you work, the strands will probably lengthen. Nip and tuck the second end in the same way as the first end. Place the finished loaf on a greased baking sheet, cover it with oiled plastic wrap, and let rise in a warm place for about 40 minutes. Meanwhile, heat the oven to 400°F.

5 Brush the loaf with the beaten egg and bake in the center of the oven for 35-45 minutes. Cool on a wire rack.

VIENNA BREAD

Vienna was in the forefront of European baking, not just for sweet pastries, chocolate cakes, and delicacies like croissants (whose crescent shape is a memento of the defeat of the Turks at the siege of Vienna), but for its bread as well.

Makes 4 loaves

* 2 cakes (30 g) fresh yeast
* 2¹/₄ cups (525 ml) very cold water
* 7¹/₂ cups (900 g) unbleached white bread flour
* 1 tablespoon salt
* ¹/₄ cup (30 g) powdered milk
* 2 tablespoons (30 g) butter

1 Cream the yeast in the water. Mix the flour, salt, and milk powder in a bowl and cut in the butter. Make a well in the center and add the liquid. Mix to form a dough, which should be moist but not wet. Turn onto a floured work surface and knead energetically for at least 10 minutes.

2 Let the dough rise in a bowl, covered with oiled plastic wrap, in a warm place (70°F) for at least 3 hours. Every hour, punch down the dough in the bowl and replace the plastic wrap. This encourages high expansion.

Every hour, punch down the dough in the bowl, then replace the plastic wrap.

3 When the dough is risen, divide it into four pieces and shape them into balls. Let them rest, covered and protected from drafts, at the side of the table for 15 minutes. Shape each of them into an oblong form by flattening the ball of dough with your hand, turning the left and right sides in to meet in the center, and sealing the joint.

4 Roll up the oblong cushions by turning with both hands, sealing the seam with the backs of your thumbs as you roll. Then extend the length of each loaf by rolling and stretching with the flat of both hands. It is best to make this shape in stages, working each loaf stage by stage, and letting each rest while working with the others. This will prevent the dough from tearing.

5 Once molded into shape, place the loaves seam-side down directly on greased and warmed baking sheets, or in floured rising baskets seam-side up. Cover with oiled plastic wrap to prevent a skin from forming. Let rise at 85°F for about 1 hour, or until they have doubled in size. Meanwhile, heat the oven to 450°F.

6 When the loaves have risen, turn them onto warmed and greased baking sheets if you used rising baskets. Slash them four times in slanting diagonals, as for a French stick. Bake on the upper rack in the oven, spraying water into the oven from an atomizer at least three times in the first 5 minutes. Bake for 20 minutes. If you have to bake on two racks, switch the sheets halfway through the cooking time, unless you have a convection oven. If at the end of the cooking time the loaves are not golden-crusted and hollow sounding when tapped, bake for another 10-15 minutes.

AUSTRIAN GUGELHUPF

Kugelhopf

This sweet yeast bread, very similar to the French brioche, is found in a broad belt of Europe, stretching from Alsace (where it is kugelhopf) to Vienna (where they say gugelhupf) and beyond. The word *kugel* is German for "ball," and a round Jewish pudding was also called by that name. Whether in the West or the East, the shape is not so much a ball as an inverted decorated bowl with a hole down the middle.

Makes 1 large loaf

* 4 tablespoons (60 g) unsalted butter for the mold

The sponge

* 1 cake (15 g) fresh yeast
* $^1/_2$ cup (120 ml) tepid milk
* $^3/_4$ cup + 1 tablespoon (120 g) unbleached all-purpose flour

The dough

* $^1/_2$ cup (120 g) unsalted butter
* 7 tablespoons (90 g) sugar
* 2 whole eggs
* 2 egg yolks
* grated zest of 1 lemon
* $^1/_2$ teaspoon salt
* 1$^1/_2$ cup (225 g) unbleached all-purpose flour
* $^3/_4$ cup (120 g) raisins, soaked in dry white wine

To finish

* confectioner's sugar for dusting

Beat the mixture, lifting and pulling until the dough is workable. Add the raisins and knead to spread them throughout the dough.

1 Chill a large gugulhupf mold in the refrigerator. Melt the 4 tablespoons butter and let it cool but not set. Brush the inside of the mold all over with the melted butter. Return the mold to the refrigerator to set, then brush again. Keep cool.

2 To make the sponge, cream the yeast in the warm milk, add the flour, and mix to make a sponge. Leave in a covered bowl at room temperature overnight.

3 To make the dough, cream the butter and sugar together with a wooden spoon. Add the eggs and yolks, lemon zest, and salt, and beat until well combined. Beat in the flour. Add the sponge to this mixture and mix to incorporate. Beat vigorously with your hand, stretching the dough as much as you can by lifting and pulling. Add a little extra flour to make the dough workable, pulling it away from the sides of the bowl. Give at least 500 strokes. Knead in the raisins.

4 Cover the bowl with oiled plastic wrap and let the dough rise in a warm place (80°F) for 1 $^1/_2$ hours, or until doubled in size. Turn onto a lightly floured surface, punch down, and put in the mold (which it should half fill), cover with oiled plastic wrap and let rise at 80°F for about 30 minutes, until it has reached the top of the mold. Meanwhile, heat the oven to 400°F.

5 Bake the bread for about 30 minutes before testing with a skewer to see if it is cooked: insert the skewer into the center, if it comes out clean, the bread is done. Cooking time will depend on the shape of the mold. Unmold and cool on a wire rack. Dust with confectioner's sugar.

SWEDISH FLAT RYE BREAD

Rågbröd

This bread is quite sensational. Made into a thin sandwich with fresh butter and a sharp, sweet jam, it is every child's after-school delight. The Swedes make other fragrant rye breads, for instance the limpa, flavored with orange peel, cumin, and other spices. These round flatbreads keep for a long time, their central holes useful for stringing them together and hanging them to dry in the rafter of the kitchen.

Makes 3 small loaves

* $1^1/_2$ cups (350 ml) milk
* 2 tablespoons (30 g) butter
* 2 tablespoons dark molasses
* $4^1/_4$ cups (425 g) wholegrain rye flour
* 1 cake (15 g) fresh yeast
* $1^1/_4$ cups (150 g) unbleached white bread flour
* 1 teaspoon salt
* 1 teaspoon ground fennel seeds

1 Warm the milk in a pan and melt the butter in it. Leave until lukewarm (110°F), then stir in the molasses. Put half the rye flour into a bowl and pour in the liquid. Crumble in the yeast and stir vigorously, then gradually add the rest of the flours, mixing all the while. Finally, add the salt and the ground fennel. Once well mixed, knead briefly in the bowl.

2 Cover the bowl with oiled plastic wrap and let the dough rise in a warm place (80°F) for about 3 hours.

3 Turn onto a lightly floured work surface and knead for 5 minutes. The dough will be firm but sticky. Keep your hands clean and moist, and scrape the work surface periodically.

4 Divide the dough into thirds and mold the pieces into balls. Flatten them with a rolling pin into 8 inch disks. Lay them on a greased baking sheet, prick all over with the tines of a fork, and cut a hole in the center with a small cookie cutter. Cover with oiled plastic wrap and let rise at 80°F for about 45 minutes, until doubled in size. Meanwhile, heat the oven to 375°F.

5 Bake the loaves for about 25 minutes. When cooked, they will be light brown and sound hollow when tapped. Brush the tops with water and cool on a rack, each loaf wrapped in a clean dish towel to keep the crust soft.

Left: *Finnish Easter Bread*
Right: *Swedish Flat Rye Bread*

FINNISH EASTER BREAD

Country life in Finland can never have been easy due to the climate. It is small wonder, therefore, that Finnish breads were often made to last. There is a wonderful variety to them, kept alive by many self-sufficient and conservative home bakers (towns and villages were too sparse for there to be much of a professional baking trade), ranging from the unleavened barley and oat breads of the north, and the softer rye breads of the eastern regions, to the dried disks of the west.

Festivities called for their own special loaves, and this Easter loaf made with yogurt is baked as a hemisphere, a common festive shape, enriched with raisins and nuts, and sweetened with a malt glaze. Perhaps to mark the fact it was a holiday, the bread was often a wheat and barley loaf, not everyday rye. As the shape is difficult to create using implements commonly found on the kitchen shelf, I suggest you make it in a well-greased 2^1/$_2$-quart pan, saucepan, or even a large cake pan, and cut it like a cake.

Makes 1 loaf

The sponge
* 1 cake (15 g) fresh yeast
* ^{1}/$_2$ cup (120 ml) plain yogurt
* ^{1}/$_2$ cup (120 ml) hot water at 130°F
* 1 cup (120 g) unbleached white bread flour

The dough
* 4 tablespoons (60 g) butter
* 2 tablespoons dark brown sugar
* 3 egg yolks
* grated zest of 1 orange
* grated zest of ^{1}/$_2$ lemon
* 1 teaspoon ground cardamom
* 1 cup + 2 tablespoons (120 g) barley flour
* scant 2 cups (225 g) unbleached white bread flour
* 1 teaspoon salt

* 3 tablespoons golden raisins
* 2 tablespoons slivered almonds
* 3 tablespoons malt extract for glaze

1 To make the sponge, cream the yeast in the yogurt and water, then mix in the flour, stirring until smooth. Let stand, covered, for 2 hours at 75°F.

2 To make the dough, melt the butter with the brown sugar, cool slightly, remove from the heat, and add the yolks. Stir this into the sponge together with the zests and spice. Combine the flours and the salt and add gradually to make a dough. Knead well on a floured surface for 10 minutes.

3 Flatten the dough on the table with the palms of your hands and spread the fruit and nuts over the surface. Roll up and knead briefly to spread them throughout the dough. Let the dough rise in a bowl, covered with oiled plastic wrap, in a warm place (80°) for approximately 1 hour, until doubled in size.

4 Turn onto a lightly floured work surface and punch down. Mold into a ball, then flatten to the approximate diameter of a greased and slightly warmed saucepan or round cake pan. It should come to no more than half the height of the container. Cover the top with oiled plastic wrap and let rise at 80°F, out of any draft. Meanwhile, heat the oven to 350°F.

5 Bake the loaf for about 1 hour, until a fine skewer inserted into the center comes out clean. Leave it to rest in the pan for 10-15 minutes before unmolding onto a wire rack to cool. Melt the malt extract and brush it all over the crust.

RUSSIAN BLACK BREAD

Mix all the ingredients for the leaven in a bowl and leave in a warm place (75°F) for 15-24 hours.

Elena Molokhovets, the Fannie Farmer of Czarist Russia, wrote of making bread on a country estate: of keeping sourdough cultures alive from one baking to the next simply by not washing out the wooden troughs in which the dough was mixed; of drying flours in front of the fire before they could be used to make bread; of putting white loaves to rise in a tub of cold water—when the loaves rise to the surface, they are ready for the oven; and of making wheat loaves with skim milk or yogurt, but rye bread with water.

"Black" bread—which was the food of peasants rather than princes—may have been more brown than black, and may have contained wheat as well as rye. Its sourness was sweetened by molasses, which also gave it color. This recipe uses toasted bread crumbs, again to give color, but also to make a lighter loaf. In Germany, it is common practice among professional bakers to recycle stale rye bread in this way.

Makes 1 loaf

The leaven
* 2 cups (200 g) wholegrain rye flour
* $^7/_8$ cup (200 ml) warm water
* 2 tablespoons of rye starter (see German Sourdough Rye Bread, page 76)

The dough
* $^1/_4$ cup (60 ml) dark molasses
* 1 cup (250 ml) hot water
* 1 cake (15 g) fresh yeast
* $1^1/_4$ cups (120 g) fine rye bread crumbs, toasted
* $^1/_4$ teaspoon ground ginger
* 1 teaspoon ground caraway seeds
* 2 cups (200 g) wholemeal rye flour
* $1^3/_4$ cups (200 g) wholemeal wheat flour
* 2 teaspoons salt

1 Mix all the ingredients for the leaven together in a bowl and leave in a warm place (75°F) for 15-24 hours.

2 To make the dough, dissolve the molasses in the hot water, then add the yeast. Add the bread crumbs and the spices, and mix together. Let stand for 30 minutes. Add the leaven, then the flours mixed with the salt. Mix to form a dough, then turn onto a floured work surface and knead for 10 minutes. Do not make the dough too stiff.

3 Let the dough rise in a bowl, covered with oiled plastic wrap, in a warm place (75°F) for 2 hours, until doubled in size. Turn onto a lightly floured work surface, punch down, and mold into a round loaf. Let rise on a warmed greased baking sheet, covered with oiled plastic wrap, at 80°F, for about 45 minutes. Do not overrise. Meanwhile, heat the oven to 450°F.

4 Slash the bread with a small cross on the top. Bake for 15 minutes, spraying the oven with water from an atomizer two or three times in the first 5 minutes. Reduce the oven temperature to 400°F and bake for 30-45 minutes more. The bread is cooked when it sounds hollow when tapped on the base. Cool on a wire rack.

AMERICAN BREADS

The United States is both a melting-pot of the world's peoples, and a bread basket. As each wave of immigrants laps the shore, they bring their food culture and their breads. Things that have almost lapsed in their place of origin, such as bagels and pretzels, suddenly crop up with greater force and popularity in the USA. This diversity makes the breads of America especially interesting.

America became the world's wheat source once the prairies had been colonized. American spring wheat makes wonderfully light bread, and American bakers enthusiastically adopted the idea of lightness, and combined it with a certain affection for sweetness, so that everyday breads sometimes lacked any character at all. This has been changing recently as young American bakers are readopting some of the traditional European methods and exploring the creation of longer process breads and loaves with fuller, more bread-like flavor. There is now a vigorous group of new-wave bakeries offering sourdoughs and traditional breads of great quality, as well as more innovative recipes that combine flavors and ingredients that would never have occurred to earlier tradesmen.

Clockwise from center: New England Buttermilk Rolls, San Francisco Sourdough, Southern Cornbread, San Francisco Sourdough, Boston Brown Bread.

SAN FRANCISCO SOURDOUGH

The pioneers who marched westwards, who followed the trail into the vast prairie, or eagerly set forth to pan for gold in California or the Yukon, were hardly able to rely on bakers and grocery stores for an ounce or two of yeast. They took their own leavening: a smidgeon of dough kept back from the last baking that could be reactivated for the next. If it was stored deep inside a sack of flour, it was safe from frosts, heatwaves, even Indian attacks!

So it was that they were called "sourdoughs," but only those who got as far as San Francisco who were to be able to make this specific sourdough, which develops its tang from the particular bacilli that seem to be partial to the air in the Bay Area. Everyone's air is different, so a true San Francisco sourdough may be impossible to repeat elsewhere, as the leaven will take on different microbes and wild yeasts, depending on the kitchen, bakery, and climate.

If you have no leaven from previous baking, see the instructions for making a sourdough leaven on page 16.

Makes 2 round loaves

The leaven
* *¹/₄ cup (60 ml) cold water*
* *walnut of leaven from previous baking*
* *1 cup (120 g) stoneground wholewheat flour*
* *pinch of ground cumin*

The sponge
* *1¹/₂ cups (350 ml) warm water*
* *1 cake (15 g) fresh yeast*
* *3¹/₂ cups (425 g) unbleached white bread flour*

The dough
* *2¹/₂ cups (300 g) unbleached white bread flour*
* *2 teaspoons salt*
* *¹/₂ teaspoon baking soda*

1 To make the leaven, mix the water with the walnut of leaven. Add the wholewheat flour and cumin, and knead to form a homogenous dough with your fingertips. Put it in a small bowl covered with plastic wrap and let it ripen in a warm place (75°F) for 6-9 hours. It will at least double in size.

2 To make the sponge, mix the leaven with the water and the yeast to make a soup, then add the flour gradually, beating all the while. Give it at least 500 beats with your hand to stretch the gluten. Let rise in a covered bowl at 70°F for at least 2 hours, but up to 12 hours. The longer it is left, the sourer it should be.

3 Mix the flour for the dough with the salt and baking soda, then add it to the sponge. Mix to form a dough, then turn onto a floured work surface and knead very well for 10-15 minutes, until it leaves the surface clean.

4 Divide the dough in half and mold each piece into a ball. Place them on a large slightly warmed and greased baking sheet, or two if your oven is not big enough to take a large baking sheet. Cover with oiled plastic wrap and let rise and spread in a warm place (80°F) for 1 ¹/₂ hours. Meanwhile, heat the oven to 450°F.

5 Slash the loaves with cuts radiating from the center, dust with flour, and bake for 25 minutes, spraying the oven with water twice in the first 4 minutes. Reduce the temperature to 400°F and bake for about 15 minutes more, until the loaves sound hollow when tapped on the base. If the loaves spread and touch each other when risen on a single baking sheet, you can easily break them apart and check more reliably that they are cooked by pressing a finger into the exposed crumb. If the indentation does not spring back, they need more cooking. Cool the loaves on wire racks.

BOSTON BROWN BREAD

The early settlers of New England found growing wheat difficult: rye was quicker and easier in wet, northerly climates. And corn, the indigenous staple of North America, was easier still. Hence breads were often made of mixed flours—as they had been among poorer households back in England rye and wheat, for instance, or the "thirded," breads made of wheat, rye, and cornmeal.

Boston Brown Bread is one of the latter, and it is steamed, betraying its origins in kitchens that had no ovens.

It is almost universal today to make Boston Brown Bread with baking soda (which was not used until the second half of the 19th century) rather than yeast, and a healthy addition of molasses. This makes it an aerated cake rather than bread as we understand it. It does go awfully well with Boston baked beans—another heavily sweetened savory food.

To make this bread, it is traditional to use a 5-cup capacity can, emptied of coffee, baked beans, or tomatoes, washed and well greased.

I favor a straight-sided 5-cup glass flask from a coffee maker. Grease the can or flask well with butter, and fit a disk of buttered parchment paper on the bottom before you put in the dough.

You will also need a small rack or trivet to keep the can or flask from touching the bottom of the saucepan and, of course, a saucepan with a lid large enough to do the steaming.

Makes 1 loaf
* *3/4 cup (90 g) cornmeal*
* *scant 1 cup (90 g) wholegrain rye flour*
* *3/4 cup (90 g) wholewheat flour*
* *1/2 teaspoon salt*
* *3/4 teaspoon baking soda*
* *1/2 teaspoon cream of tartar*
* *1 cup (225 ml) milk and water, mixed half and half*
* *6 tablespoons (90 ml) dark molasses*

1 Mix the cornmeal, rye and wheat flours, salt, baking soda, and cream of tartar together in a bowl. Warm the milk and water and dissolve the molasses in it. Add the liquid to the flour mixture and mix together with a wooden spoon to form a moist dough.

2 Grease a 5-cup capacity can or glass flask and line the bottom with a disk of parchment paper. Grease the paper and spoon the dough into the mold. It should be just over half-full. Cover the top of the mold with a double layer of waxed paper, tied securely with a piece of string.

3 Lower it onto a trivet or rack standing in a large pan. Half fill the pan with hot water. Cover with a lid and bring to a boil. Steam for about 2 1/2 hours, checking periodically to make sure the pan has not boiled dry.

4 Once the bread is cooked, take the can out of the water and turn it upside-down on a wire rack. After a minute or two, if you have greased it well enough and there are no obstructions or top lips, the loaf will drop down of its own accord. Remove the can and let the bread cool on the rack. The bread should be eaten fresh.

NEW ENGLAND BUTTERMILK ROLLS

These little rolls have the finest crumb imaginable: perfect for a dinner party, as light as air, and not difficult to make. Small wonder that they have become popular in Old England as well as in their original home, made by cooks wanting a bread suitable to go with rich and elaborate food. The instructions for making up the rolls may seem complex, but once mastered, they are easily repeated.

1 Crumble the yeast into the buttermilk, dissolve the honey in the mixture, and let ferment in a warm place for 30 minutes.

2 Melt half the butter. Combine the flour, baking soda, and salt in a bowl, and add the liquid and melted butter. Mix to form a soft dough, then turn onto a floured work surface and knead for about 8 minutes, until perfectly smooth and resilient. Let the dough rise in a bowl, covered with oiled plastic wrap, in a warm place (80°F) for about 1 hour, until doubled in size.

3 Turn onto a lightly floured work surface, punch down and form a square cushion. Let it rest, covered, for 10 minutes. Roll the dough into an oblong shape, about 20 inches long and 12 inches wide. To avoid tearing the dough, work slowly, with breaks, to give the gluten a chance to relax; otherwise, it will constantly be trying to spring back to its original size.

4 Melt the rest of the butter and brush it over the surface of the dough. Slice the dough lengthwise into six 2-inch strips. Lay these strips on top of each other, flipping the top one over so that the butter side contacts the one below.

5 Cut this strip into eight squares. Pinch one edge of each square firmly together between work surface and thumb, then place each roll, pinched side down, in the greased cup of a shallow muffin or popover pan. Cover the pan with a large inverted bowl, and let the dough rise in a warm place for 1 hour. Meanwhile, heat the oven to 450°F.

6 Bake the rolls for 15 minutes, until golden brown, then cool them on a wire rack.

Pinch one edge of each square of dough firmly together between work surface and thumb, then place each roll, pinched side down, in a greased cup of a shallow muffin or popover pan.

Makes 8 rolls

* 1 cake (15 g) fresh yeast
* $^7/_8$ cup (200 ml) buttermilk (or plain yogurt and water mixed half and half) at 100°F
* $^1/_2$ teaspoon honey
* 4 tablespoons (60 g) butter
* 3 cups (375 g) unbleached white bread flour
* $^1/_2$ teaspoon baking soda
* $^1/_2$ teaspoon salt

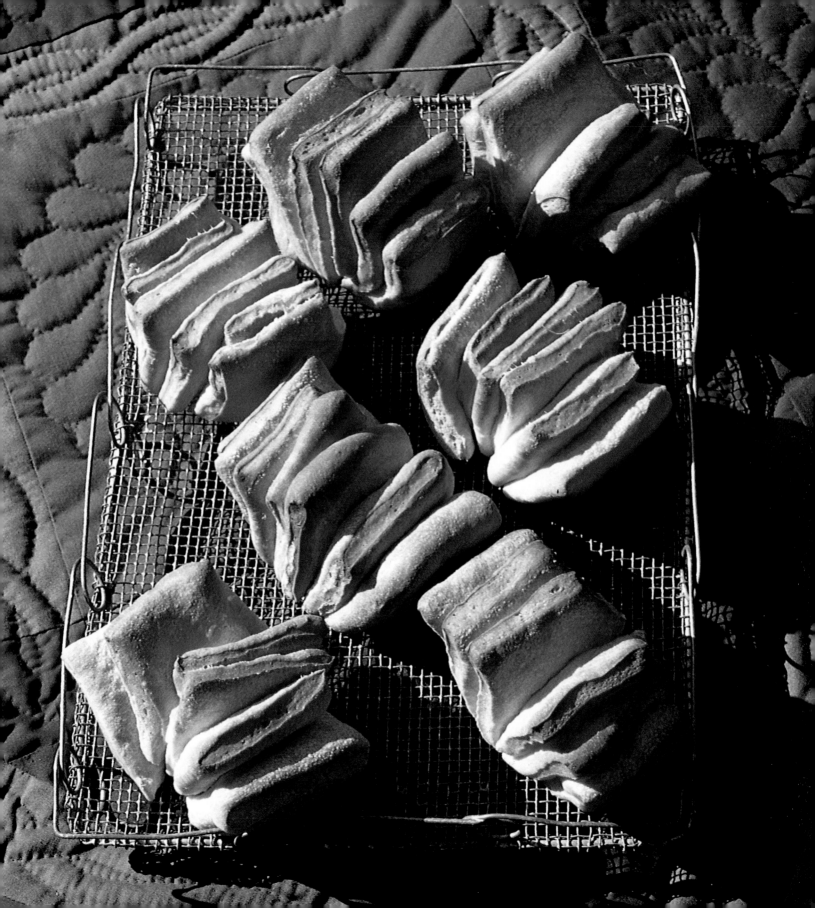

SOUTHERN CORNBREAD

When the first European settlers arrived in North America, the native Indians had corn as their staple, a grain unheard of in Europe. The settlers took to this "Indian corn" as readily as their Spanish predecessors did in Mexico and the lands to the south. The adoption of Indian methods and recipes, and their alteration to match European practice, has given us some enjoyable loaves.

Soon the settlers were making corn pone (from the Algonquin *appone*) and Johnnycakes (perhaps named after the Shawnee tribe) just as often as breads made from grains they had brought with them across the ocean.

Some recipes combined the old with the new— "ryaninjun" is rye and Indian corn—others mixed cornmeal with eggs to make almost a soufflé, and called it spoon bread. This particular recipe is as simple as can be, and is perfect served hot with bacon in the morning.

The southern states prefer a white cornmeal, and would rather have their breads cooked thin, while in the north, yellow is the favorite, and thicker is better. Color aside, there is no important difference between white and golden cornmeal.

Cornmeal has no gluten at all. It will not rise or stretch like a wheaten or even a rye dough. This is why it is mixed with other grains to make a more conventional loaf, for instance Portuguese Cornbread, page 74. The alternative is a flat bread, made lighter with eggs or baking powder, or a combination of the two.

Makes one 9-inch bread
* *1 1/4 cups (150 g) medium or fine cornmeal (see Note)*
* *1 teaspoon baking powder*
* *1/2 teaspoon salt*
* *1 egg*
* *1 cup (250 ml) milk*
* *bacon fat for greasing the skillet*

1 Heat the oven to 450°F and heat a 9-inch ovenproof skillet.

2 Mix the cornmeal, baking powder, and salt together in a bowl. Mix the egg with the milk and pour the mixture onto the cornmeal. Stir to incorporate, then beat well to be sure the batter is absolutely smooth.

3 Grease the warmed skillet with bacon fat, and pour in the batter. Return the skillet to the oven and bake the bread for about 15 minutes, until golden.

4 Slip the cooked bread out of the skillet, slice it, and eat hot with crisp bacon.

Note: The fineness of the cornmeal makes a difference in this recipe. If you can only locate coarse meal, or that sold for polenta in the Italian style, make it finer by grinding it in your spicemill or coffee grinder.

OTHER BREADS

The idea of the large, risen loaf is unique to Europe and associated cultures. The rest of the world tends to eat rice or some other staple, or cook breads that are flat even though they are leavened. One exception is the steamed bread of northern China. Otherwise, yeasted loaves have only been baked as a result of exposure to Europeans.

Flatbreads like pitta, naan, chapatis, or parathas are delicious, and should be made as often as other sorts by the keen experimenter.

The means by which they are cooked may be more difficult to replicate—not everyone has a tandoor oven in their kitchen. Equally, there are grains and materials that are virtually unobtainable outside their own countries—the fresh masa that is made into tortillas, or the *te'f* flour that is the basis of the Ethiopian injera, are two examples. In these cases, some approximation is necessary, though the results will be no less enjoyable.

Clockwise from center top: *Ethiopian Wheaten Flatbread, Pita Bread, Middle Eastern Lavash, Bagels, Challah.*

WEST INDIAN ROTI

After the abolition of slavery, the English plantations in the West Indies looked to other parts of the Empire for cheap labor. So it was that Indians took up residence, especially in the southern islands of Trinidad and Tobago, and Guianas settled on the South American mainland. Their presence transformed the cookery of those parts: curries and pilaus were common, and masalas and East Indian spices were universal flavorings. The new Indian settlers also brought their breads, and this is the origin of the West Indian roti, a variation of chapati and paratha, the Indian flatbreads. It is used as a scoop for stews and curries, and as a bread to be eaten for its own sake. Sometimes the large roti are used as giant envelopes for a filling of curried goat, say, or the smaller ones are served whole, and pieces are torn off to dip and scoop into a bowl of food. This recipe is based on the excellent instructions in a classic of Caribbean cooking by Elisabeth Lambert Ortiz, *The Complete Book of Caribbean Cooking.*

Shape the layered quarter-circles into approximate rounds and roll out to 12- inch disks again.

Makes 4 breads

* 1¹/₂ cups (225 g) unbleached all-purpose flour, or fine chapati flour
* 1 teaspoon baking powder
* 1 teaspoon salt
* 3 tablespoons (40 g) butter
* ¹/₂ - ²/₃ cup (120-150 ml) water
* ¹/₂ cup (120 g) clarified butter, melted

1 Mix the flour, baking powder, and salt together in a bowl and cut in the butter. Make a well in the center and add ¹/₂ cup (120 ml) of the water. Mix to a dough, then add more water if necessary. It should be firm, but not too stiff. Turn the dough onto a floured work surface and knead for about 4 minutes, until it leaves the surface clean.

2 Leave in a covered bowl for 30 minutes, then turn out and knead again. Divide into four pieces, mold them into balls, and roll with a rolling pin into 12-inch disks. Brush the top surface of each disk with the melted clarified butter. Fold in half, then in half again. Cover and leave for 20 minutes.

3 Shape these layered quarter-circles into approximate rounds and roll out to 12-inch disks once more.

4 Heat a griddle or heavy castiron skillet over medium heat. Cook each roti in turn. Cook on one side for 1 minute, then flip it over (some say it is best to use a wooden spatula) to cook the other side. Brush the top with clarified butter, let it cook for 2 minutes, then brush the top again. Cook for another minute. Turn over for the last time to finish off the topside until it browns.

5 The last thing to do is to break up the surface of the roti. Put the roti on a cutting board and hit it with a rolling pin until the outside layer flakes. Store wrapped in a dish towel until ready to eat.

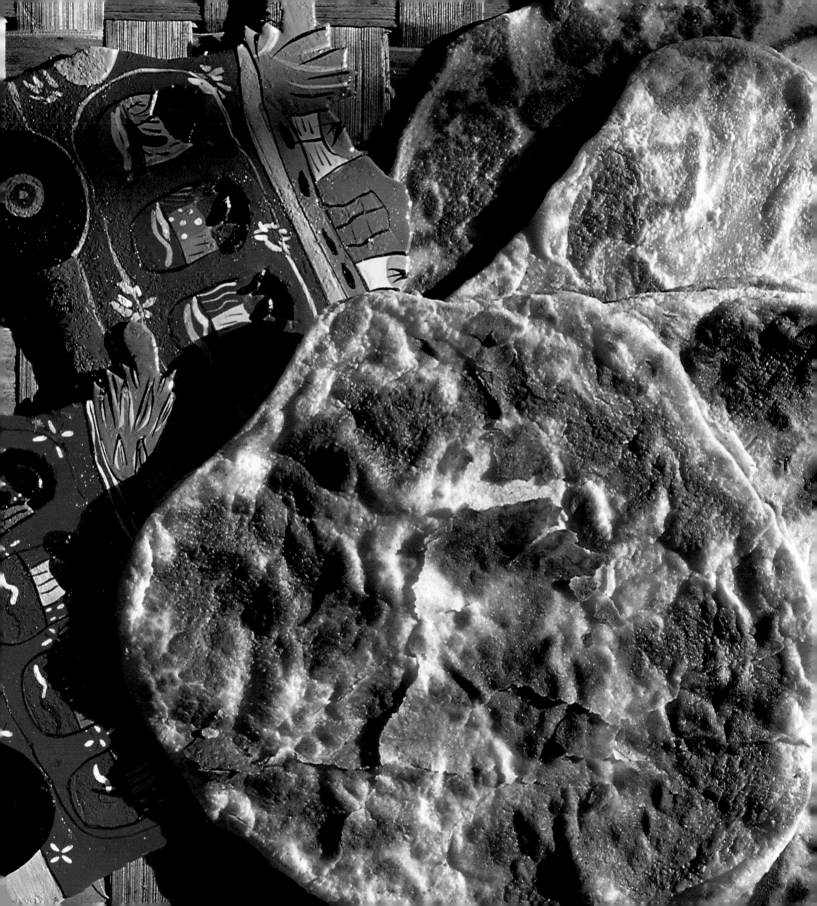

TORTILLAS

Tortillas are flat breads made from cornmeal: they are "the knife, fork, plate, and napkin" of Mexico, comments a modern scholar, "the rest [of their diet] was sauce." Tortillas were a staple of the Aztec and Maya peoples in pre-Columbian times. They developed an ingenious method of softening the dry kernels of corn by soaking and boiling them in lime-water before grinding them to a paste. This was called *nixtamal*, the raw material of fresh masa, from which tortillas are fashioned. Though it is freely available in Mexico and Latin America, fresh masa is not often exported. What we can buy is masa harina, the flour obtained by grinding after the masa has been dehydrated. It is not nearly as easy to make tortillas from masa harina as it is from fresh masa. Our efforts will not match the tortillas described by a Spanish conquistador in the 16th century that were prepared for Aztec nobles, "so thin and clean they are almost like paper and translucent."

Though Mexicans may be adept at making tortillas by slapping the dough from one hand to the other, gradually increasing the diameter of the paper-thin disk as they go, the novice will find it more difficult. One solution is to use a tortilla press, a small hand device that stamps out acceptable tortillas.

Another option is to make tortillas from wheat flour, a specialty of northern Mexico and the southwestern United States. Enthusiasts quote an Indian proverb in their favor: "After tasting flour tortillas, the children cry for them as a man craves good whiskey."

CORN TORTILLAS

Makes 12

* $1^1/_3$ cups (225 g) masa harina (corn flour)
* $1^1/_2$ cups (300 ml) tepid water

1 Mix the masina harina and water in a bowl, and bring together to form a softish dough. Getting the right

texture is all-important and will come with experience. If the dough is too wet, the tortilla will stick to hands, table, or tortilla press; if it is too dry, the dough will not hold together while you attempt to make it thin and broad. Old Latin American hands claim that the amount of water will vary according to the freshness of the masa harina, and even the state of the weather.

2 Divide the ball of dough into 12 pieces and roll these into small balls between the palms of your hands. Flatten each ball to make a small disk, then slap from hand to hand to extend it. Alternatively, place the disk on a clean surface (formica, for instance) and press it with the flat of a metal spatula, turning it over at regular intervals to ensure that it does not stick to the work surface. Continue until you achieve a tidy disk between 5 and 6 inches in diameter.

3 Heat a dry griddle over medium heat, slip the disks onto the griddle, and cook them on both sides, turning them when the edges start to curl and the surface is flecked with brown. As the tortillas cook, pile them one on the other between a clean cloth. Eat them warm (they also can be reheated).

Note: In this recipe the tortillas are not salted, but you can add a large pinch of salt to the dough if you wish.

WHEAT TORTILLAS

Makes 12

* 2 cups (300 g) unbleached all-purpose flour
* 1 1/2 teaspoons salt
* 1 1/2 teaspoons baking powder
* 4 tablespoons (60 g) lard
* 1 cup (225 ml) hot water

1 Combine the flour, salt, and baking powder in a bowl, and cut in the lard. Add the hot water and mix lightly to a soft but not runny dough. Let it rest for about 20 minutes.

2 Divide the dough into 12 pieces and mold them into balls. Cover and let rest. On a floured work surface, flatten each ball, then use a rolling pin to extend each disk to at least 6 inches. Keep turning the dough so that it does not stick to the work surface.

On a floured work surface, flatten each ball of dough, then use a rolling pin to extend each disk to at least 6 inches. Keep turning the dough so that it does not stick to the work surface.

3 Heat a dry griddle over high heat, slip the disks onto the griddle, and cook them on both sides, turning them as soon as the surface starts to bubble, after less than a minute. Stack them up in the same way as Corn Tortillas (opposite).

GUATEMALAN SWEET BUNS

Pan buns

Makes 8 large buns
* 1 cake (15 g) fresh yeast
* $^1/_2$ cup (120 ml) warm water
* 3 $^3/_4$ cups (450 g) unbleached white bread flour
* large pinch of salt
* 5 tablespoons (60 g) granulated sugar
* $^1/_2$ teaspoon ground aniseed
* $^1/_2$ cup (120 ml) coconut milk
* 8 drops of pure vanilla extract
* 1 egg
* 3 tablespoons corn oil

1 Cream the yeast in the warm water. Mix the flour, salt, sugar, and ground aniseed in a bowl, and make a well in the center. Add the yeast liquid and mix in a little of the flour with your fingers to make a sponge. Leave for 20 minutes. Add the coconut milk, vanilla, and egg to the bubbling sponge. Mix to form a dough. Add the corn oil and knead it into the dough while it is still in the bowl. Turn onto a lightly floured work surface and knead for 5 minutes.

2 Let the dough rise in a bowl, covered with oiled plastic wrap, in a warm place (75°F), until doubled in size. Turn it onto a floured work surface and divide into eight pieces. Roll these with the flat of your hands into thin sausages about 16 inches long. If the dough resists stretching, roll it in stages.

3 Shape each sausage into a spiral or snail, starting from the center and working outward. Pinch the end onto the main body of the spiral so that it does not spring out. Let the buns rise under oiled plastic wrap on a greased baking sheet for 30 minutes, until doubled in size. Meanwhile, heat the oven to 450°F. Bake the buns on the center shelf for 15-20 minutes, until evenly browned. Cool on wire racks.

PERSIAN FLATBREAD

Barbari

Makes 2 loaves
* 2 cakes (30 g) fresh yeast
* 1 cup (250 ml) warm water at 90°F
* 3 $^3/_4$ cups (450 g) white bread flour
* 1 teaspoon salt
* vegetable oil for brushing

1 Cream the yeast in the warm water. Put the flour in a bowl and make a well in the center. Pour the yeast liquid into the well. Dust a little of the flour over the surface of the liquid and let bubble in a warm place (75°F) for 20 minutes. Add the salt to the sponge mixture and mix it all into a dough. Turn onto a floured work surface and knead for 10 minutes, keeping the dough moist but not sticky.

2 Let the dough rise in a bowl, covered with oiled plastic wrap, in a warm place for about 45 minutes, until doubled in size.

3 Turn onto a lightly floured work surface and divide the dough in half. Work each piece into a ball, then roll each into a long oval about $^1/_2$ inch thick. Place the ovals on greased baking sheets, cover with oiled plastic wrap, and let rise in a warm place for 20 minutes. Meanwhile, heat the oven to 425°F.

4 Brush the loaves with oil and bake in the center of the oven for about 20 minutes, until golden brown. Eat warm.

ETHIOPIAN WHEATEN FLATBREAD

Yesinde injera

Conventional baked breads in Ethiopia are called *dabbo*, but the injera, which is a soured pancake made from various grains, is the oldest and most traditional form. The staple grain of Ethiopia is a grass unique to the country called *t'ef* (*Eragrostis Abyssinica*). The nearest approximation we can find of grains available here is millet. Different forms of millet, such as sorghum, are important staples in poorer countries in tropical Africa and Asia, although the breads made with such flour are not capable of normal leavening.

The recipe I have given here uses wheat, which is more acceptable to home bakers. Barley, millet, rice flour, or cornmeal could equally well be tried. Many recipes now use baking powder or yeast to give a start to the fermentation or aeration. I suggest using a piece of leaven to give a sour taste, as well as a piece of fermented yeast dough from any bread made the previous day, to aid fermentation.

Injera have to be made in a large skillet when baking at home. Ethiopian cooks, however, make them on a flat griddle laid over flames. The injera is laid flat on a dish and fragrant stew (*wot* or *we't*) is piled in the center for sampling by means of tearing pieces of injera from the edge and using them as scoops.

Makes about 10
* 1 tablespoon leaven (see recipe, page 16)
* 2 tablespoons of the previous day's dough
* $1^1/_2$ quarts (1.35 liters) still spring water or filtered water
* 5 cups (700 g) stoneground wheatmeal (85% extraction) flour, or equal parts unbleached all-purpose flour and wholewheat (100%) flour

1 Mix the leaven, fermented dough, and water together in a bowl. Add the flour to make a batter. Let stand at room temperature at least overnight, or up to 24 hours, until it has risen and tastes sour.

2 Heat a large nonstick skillet over medium heat. Pour about $3/_4$ cup batter into the pan in a spiral pattern, starting at the edge and working clockwise until you reach the center, then tip the pan so that the batter covers the bottom, like a pancake. Cook for 3-4 minutes. The edge will lift from the pan when it is ready. Take it out of the skillet and cool on a clean dish towel while cooking the remaining batter.

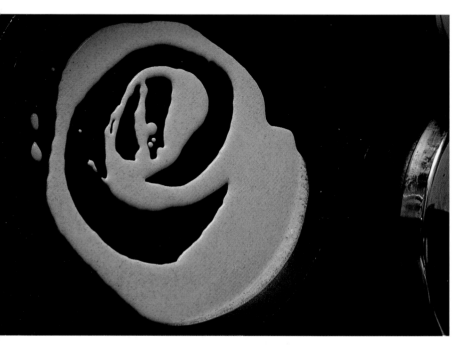

Pour approximately $3/_4$ cup of the batter into the heated skillet in a spiral pattern, starting at the edge and working clockwise until you reach the center.

109

BAGELS

The bagel is a Jewish bread, perhaps originating in Austria, then migrating to Polish Galicia, and thence to North America, where it has become a popular breakfast or lunch food. The slightly enriched dough is shaped into rings, given a short rise, then poached for a matter of seconds before baking. The poaching makes the crust chewy rather than crisp, a texture reinforced by the short rising time. The crust may be brushed with egg to give gloss (an effect also achieved by putting sugar into the poaching water), and it may be coated with onion flakes, poppy seeds, or sesame seeds.

Makes 10

* 1 cake (15 g) fresh yeast
* 2 teaspoons malt extract
* $^2/_3$ cup (150 ml) tepid water
* $2^1/_2$ cups (300 g) unbleached white bread flour
* 1 teaspoon salt
* 2 tablespoons vegetable oil
* 1 tablespoon malt extract for the poaching water
* 1 egg white mixed with 1 tablespoon cold water for glaze
* poppy seeds or sesame seeds (optional)

1 Combine the yeast, malt extract, and the tepid water in a bowl and stir to dissolve. Mix the flour and salt together, form a well in the center, and pour in the yeast liquid, then the oil. Mix to form a dough, then turn onto a floured work surface and knead for 8 minutes. The dough should be quite soft and pliable.

2 Let the dough rise in a bowl, covered with oiled plastic wrap, in a warm place (75°F) for about 1 hour, until doubled in size.

3 Turn the dough onto the work surface, divide into 10 equal sections, and roll each of them into a neat and tidy ball. Let them rest for 5 minutes, covered with a clean cloth. To form the bagels, flatten each ball slightly, then pinch your thumb through the center to the bottom. The rings can be made larger by twirling them around your thumb, or a forefinger. The hole in the middle of the bagel needs to be bigger at this stage than you want it to be at the end of cooking. As the dough rises, the hole will shrink.

4 Let rise on a floured tray covered with a cloth for 10 minutes. Heat the oven to 425°F. Bring a large saucepan containing the water and malt extract to a boil, then leave it simmering. When the bagels have risen, slip three or four into the simmering water. Poach for 1 minute, then turn with a slotted spoon and cook the other side for 30 seconds. Remove and drain on a clean dish towel.

5 Once all the bagels have been poached, place them on a greased baking sheet and brush with the egg white glaze. Bake in the oven for about 30 minutes, until golden brown.

Slip the bagels, three or four at a time, into the pan of water and malt extract. Poach for 1 minute, then turn with a slotted spoon and cook the other side for 30 seconds.

PITTA BREAD

*Top: Pitta Bread
Bottom: Middle
Eastern Lavash*

Makes 8
* 1 cake (15 g) fresh yeast
* 1 cup (225 ml) tepid water at 70°F
* 3¹/₂ cups (400 g) unbleached white bread flour
* 2 teaspoons salt
* 1 tablespoon olive oil

1 Dissolve the yeast in the water in a large bowl. Mix the flour and salt and add them gradually to the liquid, beating vigorously. Mix the dough energetically for 8-10 minutes to condition it. Add the olive oil and mix once more. Turn the dough onto a floured surface and knead for 5 minutes.

2 Let the dough rise in a bowl, covered with oiled plastic wrap, for about 1 ¹/₂ hours, until doubled in size. Turn onto a well-floured work surface. Divide the dough into eight pieces and form them into balls. Let rest for 5 minutes, then roll into flat ovals about ¹/₄ inch thick. Let them rise in a warm place, between two floured dish towels, for about 20 minutes. Meanwhile, heat the oven to 450°F and warm one or two greased baking sheets.

3 Slip the breads onto the sheet or sheets and bake for about 6 minutes. They should not color—more than one rack may be used in the oven at one time, but the heat must be intense enough to cause the dough to puff up (the result of steam forcing the two halves of the bread apart, which is one reason for the moist initial dough). Cool briefly on wire racks, then wrap the pitta in dish towels to keep the crusts soft. Eat them warm.

Variation: "Family-size" pitta breads can be made by dividing the dough into four pieces instead of eight. The cooking time will need to be slightly longer.

MIDDLE EASTERN LAVASH

Lavash is the crisp flatbread found universally throughout Arab and Near Eastern countries. It uses the same dough as naan, but it is rolled thinner so that it bakes crisp. Lavash can be made and stored like a crispbread.

Makes 6-8
* *6 oz (175 g) of the previous day's dough*
* *³/₄ cup (175 ml) plain yogurt at room temperature*
* *1 teaspoon salt*
* *¹/₂ cake (7 g) fresh yeast*
* *scant 2 cups (225 g) unbleached white bread flour*

1 Put the previous day's dough in a bowl with the yogurt, salt, and yeast. Mix with a wooden spoon until entirely smooth. Add the flour gradually, mixing vigorously to form a moist and supple dough. Turn onto a floured work surface and knead for 10 minutes.

2 Let the dough rise in a bowl, covered with oiled plastic wrap, in a warm place (75°F) for between 2 and 3 hours, until tripled in size.

3 Turn onto a lightly floured work surface, punch down lightly, and divide into six or eight pieces. Form them into balls and let rest on the side of the table. Meanwhile, heat the oven to its maximum temperature, at least 450°F, and warm two greased baking sheets.

4 Roll out each ball to an oval as thin as possible (taking into account the size of your oven). You may need to rest each piece in the middle of rolling to relax the gluten and lessen the resistance to the rolling pin. Transfer the lavash to a warm baking sheet as soon as rolling is completed, and bake, without turning, for 5-6 minutes. Cool, then wrap in a cloth before serving.

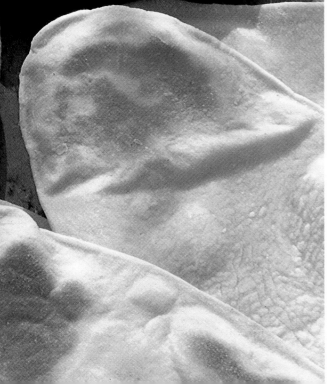

CHALLAH

Challah is bread for the Jewish sabbath: a luxury wheaten loaf to mark the holy day, set it apart from the incessant work of the rest of the week, and the daily diet of dark rye bread. Bread holds the key to much religious symbolism for Jews, as for other cultures. Challah was traditionally the dough set apart and given to the priests. This symbolic gift is still re-enacted by the breadmaker of the Jewish household, or by the Jewish commercial baker. A portion of dough is extracted before the final loaf is shaped; it is blessed and then burned to a cinder in the oven. In Middle Eastern cultures, the same ritual is thought to ward off the evil eye.

Challah is usually a braided or plaited loaf, witness perhaps to the medieval German origin of the bread we eat today, but this coiled shape is also traditional for the celebration of the Jewish New Year—its roundness symbolizing the fullness of time.

The implicit luxury of this bread is from butter and eggs (though not all recipes have these). A golden color—inside and out—is a hallmark. Some bakers add saffron to the dough to accentuate this.

Place the dough on a greased baking sheet and shape it into a simple coil, pinching the end to hold the shape in the oven.

Makes 1 large loaf

* *2 eggs mixed with enough tepid water to yield one cup (225 ml)*
* *1 tablespoon honey*
* *1 cake (15 g) fresh yeast*
* *3 ³/₄ cups (450 g) unbleached white bread flour*
* *1 teaspoon salt*
* *4 tablespoons (60 g) unsalted butter*
* *1 egg yolk beaten with a little water for glaze*
* *1 teaspoon poppy seeds or sesame seeds (optional)*

1 Put the eggs and tepid water in a bowl, add the honey and yeast, and stir to dissolve. Mix the flour and salt in a bowl and cut in the butter. Make a well in the center and pour in the yeast liquid. Mix to form a soft dough, then knead on a lightly floured work surface for 5 minutes.

2 Place the dough in a bowl with a piece of oiled plastic wrap pressed to the surface, to prevent a skin from forming, and let rise at room temperature for about 3 hours.

3 Turn onto a lightly floured work surface and knead for 5 minutes. Return the dough to the bowl, cover again, and let rise a second time in a warm place (80°F) for between 1 and 2 hours, until at least doubled in size.

4 For the final shaping, gently roll the dough into a "sausage" about 16-20 inches long, taking care not to tear the skin on the "top" side, which should show no joins from the turning and rolling. Make a simple coil, pinching the end to hold the shape in the oven. Place on a greased baking sheet, cover with oiled plastic wrap, and let rise at 80°F for about 1 hour. Meanwhile, heat the oven to 400°F.

5 Brush the loaf with the egg yolk glaze and scatter with the poppy or sesame seeds, if desired. Bake on the middle rack of the oven for 30-40 minutes. The loaf should feel very light and sound hollow when tapped. Cool on a wire rack.

NAAN

There are a host of breads from India, some leavened like this naan, others not, like chapatis and parathas. Naan is the white bread of the Muslim northwest, of Punjab and Kashmir and, beyond that, Afghanistan and central Asia. The large breads in restaurants are cooked in tandoors—beehive domes arching over a charcoal brazier on the floor of the oven, with other food being added through an opening at the top. When making bread, the cook slaps the sheet of dough onto the side wall of the tandoor. It hangs down over the flame in the pit, one end stuck to the wall, the rest forming a huge tear shape below. Households, even in India, do not usually have tandoors, so home-produced naans are cooked in a conventional oven, under a broiler, or over charcoal

The writer Helen Saberi, who lived and cooked in Afghanistan, has eloquently described naans made for her. While most recipes suggest a simple yeast dough, or sometimes a yogurt fermentation, she noticed that many Afghan naans were made with a sourdough, or at least a fermentation based on a piece of dough saved from the previous day's baking. This gives the bread an excellent sharp flavor that brings out the best taste of the flour. While Indian breads are often made with fine white flour (Indian wheat is quite strong and suitable for breadmaking), Afghani baking is usually done with finely ground wholewheat, similar to chapati flour, which could be used in this recipe.

Makes 2 large breads or 4 smaller ones
* 6 oz (175 g) of the previous day's dough, kept back, covered, in a cool place
* $^3/_4$ cup (175 ml) plain yogurt, at room temperature
* 1 teaspoon salt
* $^1/_2$ cake (7 g) fresh yeast
* scant 2 cups (225 g) unbleached white bread flour

1 Put the previous day's dough in a bowl with the yogurt, salt, and yeast. Mix with a wooden spoon until entirely smooth. Add the flour gradually, mixing vigorously until it forms a moist and supple dough. Turn it onto a floured work surface and knead for 10 minutes. Let the dough rise in a bowl, covered with oiled plastic wrap, in a warm place (75°F) for between 2 and 3 hours, until tripled in size.

2 Turn the dough onto a lightly floured work surface and punch down lightly. Divide it into two or four pieces, form them into balls, and let them rest on the side of the work surface. Meanwhile, heat the oven to 450°F (or hotter, if possible) and warm some greased baking sheets.

3 Roll out each ball to an oval about $^1/_4$ inch thick: if making two larger breads, the ovals will measure about 20 x 8 inches. You may need to rest each piece in the middle of rolling to relax the gluten and lessen the resistance to the rolling pin.

4 Transfer the naan to the baking sheets as soon as rolling is completed, and bake, without turning, for 5-8 minutes. They should color, and they may be crisp in parts. Once cooked, wrap in a cloth until needed, but eat them warm and fresh.

Variations: The naan can be brushed with ghee (clarified butter) for an extra touch of luxury, and this may be enhanced with a sprinkling of spice or seed as well.

If you would rather cook the bread under a salamander grill or broiler, you may find the smaller size more convenient to handle. Turn the breads halfway through the cooking unless you are using a heavy castiron grill pan that can be preheated.

ACKNOWLEDGMENTS

I am grateful to Elizabeth Carter, Rolf Peter Weichold, Adam Nicholson, Angelika Noack, Crowdy Mill of Harbertonford, and many others for advice and assistance.

SELECT BIBLIOGRAPHY

Banfield, Walter: Manna (London, 1937)

Bateman, Michael, & Heather Maisner: The Sunday Times Book of Real Bread (Aylesbury, 1982)

Bürher, E. M., & W. Zehr: Le pain à travers les ages (Paris, 1985)

Calvel, R.: La Boulangerie Moderne (3rd edition, Paris, 1962)

Clayton, Bernard, Jr.: Bernard Clayton's New Complete Book of Breads (New York, 1987)

Collister, Linda, & Anthony Blake: The Bread Book (London, 1993)

Confederation Nationale de la Boulangerie: Mon Métier Boulanger (Paris, 1990)

David, Elizabeth: English Bread and Yeast Cookery (London, 1977)

Duff, Gail: The Complete Bread Book (London, 1993)

Edlin, A.: A Treatise on the Art of Bread-Making (London, 1805, reprinted 1992)

Field, Carol: The Italian Baker (New York, 1985)

Irons, J. R.: Breadcraft (n.d., ca.1935)

Kelly, Sarah: Festive Baking In Austria, Germany and Switzerland (Harmondsworth, 1985)

Kirkland, John: The Modern Baker, Confectioner and Caterer (London 1907)

Littlewood, Alan: Breadcraft (London, 1987)

Mesfin, D. J.: Exotic Ethiopian Cooking (Falls Church, Virginia, 1993)

Montandon, J.: Le bon pain des provinces de Frances (Lausanne, 1979)

Ortiz, Joe: The Village Baker (Berkeley, 1993)

Parmentier, Antoine Auguste: Le Parfait Boulanger (edition of 1788, Paris; reprinted Marseille, 1981)

Poilâne, Lionel: Faire son pain (Paris, 1982)

Poilâne, Lionel: Guide de l'amateur de pain (Paris, 1981)

Time-Life Books: Breads (Amsterdam, 1980)

INDEX